THE

WHITE IMPALA

The Story of a Game Ranger

By

NORMAN CARR

With a Foreword by
Prince Bernhard of the Netherlands

COLLINS
St James's Place, London
1969

599.096894

© *Norman Carr, 1969*
Printed in Great Britain
by Cox & Wyman Ltd.,
London, Fakenham and Reading

To
JUDY, PAMELA AND ADRIAN
whose well-being I have neglected
in my pursuit of adventure in out-of-the-way places

FOREWORD

I have known Mr. Norman Carr's long and outstanding work in the field of wildlife for some time, and after reading his *Return to the Wild* I hoped it might be possible to visit him in the Luangwa Valley. It was therefore with considerable regret that recently I had to postpone the safari which we had planned together.

The more so because *The White Impala* has given me an extraordinarily vivid impression of the magnificent wildlife resources of Luangwa and the Zambian sanctuaries – and of some of the problems confronting the author and other conservationists who are struggling to save the fauna of Africa and their habitat. I therefore hope that a great many people will read this book so that they can share in the author's adventures – some exciting, others amusing – and enjoy his fascinating observations of the natural world.

Although one cannot fail to be impressed by Mr. Carr's close affinity with the animals about which he writes so well, his approach to the problems of conservation is realistic rather than sentimental and his remarkable career not only confirms the old dictum that the best gamekeeper is a converted poacher, but also illustrates the new approach to conservation which has evolved in our lifetime.

Ultimately, it is public opinion which will influence the fate of the world's wild life, and while we cannot all visit Africa to formulate our views, we can all derive both information and pleasure from a book such as this one.

Bernhard
The Prince of the Netherlands,
President,
The World Wildlife Fund

CONTENTS

ENLIGHTENMENT

CONSERVATIONIST

EPILOGUE

LIST OF ILLUSTRATIONS

MAP

PROLOGUE

1. Off the map

Early in life my imagination was fired by stories of intrepid hunters and explorers who opened up Central Africa during the pioneer days of colonisation. My youthful mind invested these legendary heroes with supernatural qualities. Automatically, I assumed that they descended from their Olympian heights only, if at all, between glorious prolonged hunting trips. It made no difference that, to my father, many of them were ordinary men – his friends – who settled down to discuss their latest adventures with the same enthusiastic readiness as they pursued their prey. They were my gods and I listened to them spellbound.

I was born in 1912 in Chinde, which is on a delta in the mouth of the Zambezi, and spent the first seven years of my life there. Looking back, what I recall most vividly was that time of day when the sun sank slowly and people came to life after their torpid midday siesta. I remember the cool gentle breeze blowing in from the Indian Ocean, the beautiful piercing sunsets. In the evenings, after the scorching sandy roads had had time to cool down, my mother would take me and my sister Evelyn for pleasant leisurely walks. Invariably we would meet neighbours, join forces with them and idle the time away. Sundown found us all either at their house or ours.

Then, for the next hour or so, we children would be completely forgotten while our parents gossiped and enjoyed the inevitable sundowners, which were, and still are, part of the social tradition of Africa. When the conversation turned to the latest hunting adventure of someone newly arrived from up-country I would listen eagerly, silently – hoping to postpone the awful moment when one of the grown-ups would inconsiderately remember it was time all children were in bed. Then I would lie awake, straining my ears to catch snatches of a conversation two rooms away, until, eventually, I was forced to give up and listen instead to the vibrant night sounds of Africa.

Bedtime was always strongly associated with the incessant chirping of crickets and the croaking of frogs – particularly the frogs. Even now, the sound of frogs at night brings back memories of lying in bed in Chinde, thinking of the wonders and mysteries of the world and of all the exciting things grown-ups could do. As I lay awake, listening to this wild orchestra, I vowed that one day I myself would be a hunter. I prayed that Africa would not be totally discovered before I was old enough to explore it – that there would be some corner left for me to find.

Chinde was a settlement of wooden houses built on stilts in a tropical mangrove swamp in the Zambezi delta. The only justification for its existence was its terminal position on the sea coast where the paddle-steamers, which plied their way up and down the Zambezi, could tie up and collect cargo for the return journey inland. For Chinde did not boast a harbour. The sand-bars, formed by the silt carried down by the river, prevented any of the small sea-going coastal steamers from coming into port; they were forced to anchor out at sea. Their cargo was laboriously off-loaded into lighters and then transferred into the noisy paddle-steamers which splashed and panted an asthmatical course deep into the interior. Chinde, however, was the gateway to the hinterland and thus, for me at least, very exciting, for the hinterland spelt adventure and a challenge which one day I was determined to take up.

Although it was in Portuguese territory, a small section of Chinde was set aside as a British Concession where goods, destined for the British territories of Rhodesia and Nyasaland, could be bonded during trans-shipment to overcome elaborate customs formalities. My father was one of a small group of Englishmen living in this fenced-in concession and concerned with the handling of supplies in transit to these inland territories.

One of my earliest memories is of a journey up the Zambezi in a stern-wheel paddle-steamer. Lashed to each side was a large barge, extending the whole length of the steamer, crowded with jabbering native passengers. It must have been during the dry season when the river was low, for I remember the main stream of the river meandering between innumerable sand-banks on which, occasionally, we would see basking crocodiles. At every sweep of the main channel the boat would run aground on one of the sandbanks. Then there would be pan-demonium as a dozen or more of the native crew, dressed in blue sailor jumpers and shorts, leapt waist-deep into the water and shoved and heaved, while the skipper shouted instructions and abuse at them from the upper deck, until finally the boat was dislodged from the sandbank. On either side of the river, tall elephant grass stretched monotonously away into the dis-tance as far as the eye could see. Only sometimes in the course of our journey did we come across a native settlement: a few untidy reed shelters scattered among the trees with just enough land above flood level in which to cultivate an occasional small garden.

As we drew near, men, women and naked piccanins waved

and gesticulated from a great distance, exchanging greetings with the horde of passengers in the barges. As the gap between our boat and the shore narrowed their voices grew correspondingly louder. The jabbering was deafening. The lack of vocabulary in Bantu language is more than compensated for by volume. Where, among Europeans, the inarticulate depend upon profanity to give themselves a feeling of eloquence, these people merely turn up the volume to achieve the same effect.

On board with us was a Scotsman, referred to by everyone as 'Mac'. He was a huge giant of a man, with a red beard and a gentle, purring voice. I clearly remember him and his energetic *capitao*, who had come down to Chinde to meet him, supervising the loading of equipment into the holds of one of the barges. There must have been well over a hundred boxes and bundles of every size and shape, all meticulously numbered and labelled. His half-dozen rifle cases were stacked separately on the passenger deck where he could watch them more closely. He was immediately placed high in my gallery of heroes when he took a fancy to me and told me of his hunting adventures as we sat on the top deck together, listening to the paddle-wheels pushing us rhythmically up-river. One of the things I learnt was that, having spent a year at his home in Scotland, he was returning to Africa to undertake an expedition into the gorilla country of the Congo. I wonder if he got there. Frequently in later life I tried to find out who my hero was. I never succeeded.

My last vivid recollection of Chinde was of a cyclone striking it. Suddenly the skies opened and the rain poured down in a solid flood. Blinding flashes of lightning exploded simultaneously with every crash of thunder and between each salvo a continuous rumble could be heard like a barrage of artillery in the distance. The force of the wind, which had started gently at first, built up until the crescendo of noise was un-

The author's father, with the Zambezi river-boats behind
Below, author's mother carried in a machila

Author with elephant calf he adopted during his early hunting career and, below, an elephant that decided to charge while being photographed

endurable – high-pitched like a human shriek. Giant hands seemed to push at our house, causing it to sway drunkenly until I felt it could stand no longer. Then a lull, followed by an ominous silence.

The silence was worst of all – the silence of death – as we waited for the powerful wind to strike again. We could hear it in the distance, a slight sighing at first, then a whine, then the sound increasing like some banshee whose wail portends disaster. Surely, I thought, in the next furious onslaught our house would collapse around us. I was wrong. But for two weeks the rain relentlessly persisted.

During the cyclone, my sister and I lived with my mother upstairs, but even there the floors were two feet under water. We children thought this great fun. I cannot remember seeing my father at all during the whole episode, but I suppose that like all other able-bodied men, he was out in the boats doing rescue and salvage work all day.

When the floods subsided, sea-going boats and barges were left high and dry for as far as a mile inland. Chinde never really recovered. And worse was to follow. A few years later an even more severe blow struck her, from a different quarter. This time an economic one. It was decided that a railway line should be built between Beira and Nyasaland. Chinde was to be by-passed. Before long her harbourless port had become redundant and there was no longer any justification for her existence.

So you will not find Chinde on the map. The sea and the jungle have claimed her, and the once-flourishing little settlement remains buried in the past, like the adventurers whom she served so loyally as a stepping-stone into the mysterious exciting interior.

2. Tyro

I am afraid I never took my schooling in England very seriously. I was sent there in 1920 and looked upon it as an experience to be completed as quickly and painlessly as possible so that I could return to Africa and hunting – an attitude hardly conducive to study. Hence my ten years' banishment was not crowned with scholastic glory, to the great disappointment of my parents, who had now settled in Nyasaland as tobacco planters and who expected rather better things from their eldest son. Perhaps, after all, there was some justification for the remark of one of my teachers who, clearly unfamiliar with Churchill's parody of a similar misuse of the English language, wrote of my performance in a school report: 'This pupil sets himself an abysmally low standard up to which he finds it difficult to keep.'

I was happy to leave school in 1929 and return to Africa, where much of the next few years was to be spent in the bush. My forays across the Nyasaland border into Portuguese territory became increasingly frequent, and the fact that I had no licence to hunt in this territory deterred me not at all. In fact, the knowledge that I risked severe penalties, and would undoubtedly end up in jail if caught, only added extra spice to my poaching trips. At that age any extra risk spelt excitement, and excitement was an uncontrollable challenge.

In those days there was no Game Department in Nyasaland

so, in order to exterminate elephants that were raiding the native gardens, the Government offered free licences to certain hunters to shoot as many elephants as they could provided they were tracked down from the gardens. For his services the hunter was awarded the 'ground' tusk (the one nearest the ground when the elephant fell down), while the other was to be handed in to the Boma.* This system, which was commonly used in other poorer colonies, saved the Government the expense of employing its own hunting staff. It was, however, greatly abused.

A part-time hunter going out in his free moments for sport or reward could not afford to wait around in a village for several days, or even weeks, in the hope that an elephant would decide to raid a garden. He went out, as I did, and shot the first elephant he saw with reasonable tusks and called it a garden raider. There was no way to check this and so the system was totally ineffective as a means of garden protection. In fact it had the reverse effect. The shooting of elephants miles away from cultivation could not possibly be associated with punitive measures and so it served no disciplinary purpose whatever. The rest of the herd would happily continue to raid village gardens undisturbed.

It was in the guise of crop-protector in Nyasaland, therefore, that I served the apprenticeship which qualified me for my future career. I was very proud of my fiftieth elephant, which I shot on the banks of the Shire river in the Liwonde district on my twentieth birthday.

* Nowadays the word 'Boma' (which owes its origins to the thorn boma, built round an encampment to keep out hostile lions or tribes) is used to mean a Government administrative centre. But more particularly it means the District Commissioner's office and all the services that go with it – dispensary, post office, agricultural officer's office, and so on.

My companion on some of these hunts was Archie Dayton, who worked in a bank in Blantyre. He would join me sometimes during the week-ends, or whenever he could get a few days off from the bank. I enjoyed the companionship of someone who was as keen on hunting as I was, and we would often sit up late into the night over the camp fire, discussing our adventures or theorising about the habits of wild animals. Reluctant to stop, unable to stay awake, we would wrap up in a blanket next to the fire and continue our somewhat drowsy ramblings until one of us would fall asleep and the other, finding he had no audience, quickly follow suit. We usually had a native guide and tracker with us to share the warmth of the fire. It was a simple carefree life. We could not have chosen a better classroom in which to study the environment around us, for we both had a lot to learn about the ways of wild animals. We carried with us on these trips a minimum of luggage, a surplus of enthusiasm, and a sublime ignorance of the ways of nature.

During those days there was one particularly unpleasant group of elephants, known as the Mpimbi herd, which frequented an area of thick bush between the Zomba mountain range and Balakas. They had earned a notorious reputation for chasing any hunter they scented on their tracks and had already killed at least three natives. As a result they had been outlawed by the authorities. Some years previously the Government had even sent a detachment from the Army with automatic weapons to try and eliminate them – with little success. They seemed to present us with a permanent challenge, and Archie and I decided to take them on.

We had managed to account for several of them when I was forced on one occasion to beat a hurried and undignified retreat before a screaming cow elephant who came for me in

thick cover. I was determined to recover my lost dignity. Full
of resolution, Archie and I planned to go after the Mpimbi
herd the following week-end. But fate had other plans in store
for Archie.

Just before we were due to leave, he sent me a message from
Blantyre to say that a man-eating lion had killed a villager at
Chikwawa. Would I join him on a lion-hunt instead? Perhaps
fortunately, I turned down the tempting offer as I felt I had a
personal score to settle with our friends from Mpimbi.

So Archie went off to Chikwawa, which was about fifty
miles south-west of Blantyre, with another hunting friend,
Johnny Phillips. They arrived just at sundown at Ndombo's
village, where the African had been killed. By the time they
had set up camp some distance from the village it was quite
dark, with that compelling total darkness of a moonless
African night.

Johnny and Archie were sitting round the camp fire having a
drink and planning their hunt for the morning when, without
any warning, the subject of their plotting plunged out of the
darkness into the firelight and leapt upon Archie from the rear,
grabbing him by the shoulder and dragging him away into the
night.

Johnny fell back. A terrified panic ensued. The native boys
scattered screaming. Only the cookboy showed any presence
of mind. Snatching a burning log, which helped to light up the
scene, he brandished it aloft, as Johnny rushed for his rifle and
let off a couple of rounds. Startled by the noise, the lion dropped
its victim and sloped off, while Johnny emptied his rifle in
the general direction of its retreat.

Terrified of what they would find, they followed it into the
darkness. But Archie was not only alive, he was conscious –
although severely bitten through the shoulder and with one

arm badly damaged. He was rushed to Blantyre hospital for immediate treatment, for this was before the days of antibiotics and the risk of blood-poisoning was considerable.

Physically he was lucky to recover after only a few weeks in hospital, but he was never quite the same again when tracking lion. Oddly enough the incident seemed not to have affected his nerve when hunting elephant. We had several more hunts together, though he never saw the Mpimbi again. That was left to me to settle on my own account. In fact, while the abortive lion-hunt was going on, I had managed to shoot two more from the herd, which evened the score I had against them and allowed me to recover my lost confidence.

In 1931 my father died. I had never known him really intimately. There existed between us an embarrassing shyness which no doubt emanated from our long separation when I was growing up in England. But he was a good man, generous to a degree, always ready to help anyone in poor straits, and he would give his last penny to help a friend in need. He must have had his share of the adventurous spirit to be lured to Africa in 1898, and this characteristic showed itself in his willingness to gamble his capital on any crack-brained venture his friends persuaded him to invest in. He must have been a poor judge of character or a poor businessman, I think, for these get-rich-quick schemes were seldom profitable and several of his partners ended up owing him large sums of money which he never recovered. Consequently, when he died my mother was left with very little money and it fell upon me to support the family and to keep my younger brother and sister at boarding school. This rather curtailed my vagrant hunting life, as I was compelled to settle down and take up a regular job with the Nyasaland Government, but I still managed to spend all my spare time on hunting trips.

My younger brother, Alan, who was seven years my junior, would often accompany me on these trips when he was on holiday from school. We had an old 1923 Austin Tourer which we turned into a hunting vehicle by stripping it down to the chassis and dispensing with inessential refinements such as windscreen and mudguards. We called her the 'Steamboat'. With this rugged vehicle we would take off from Zomba every Friday afternoon, hunt during the week-end, and travel back home through the night on Sunday. Steamboat was a splendidly sturdy companion and would travel over the roughest terrain, miles away from any road, into places where modern four-wheel-drive vehicles would hesitate to go.

When I eventually left Zomba I bequeathed this car to Alan and he used to run it during his holidays until the time when he got his first job. It was a familiar sight in Zomba for many years and caused a good deal of ribald comment, especially when Alan put a neat thatched roof over the driver's seat to keep out the rain.

3. The Luangwa Valley

About a year before Hitler marched on Poland I managed to get a job as Elephant Control Officer with the Government of Northern Rhodesia and was fortunate enough to be posted to Fort Jameson, with responsibility over the whole Luangwa Valley.

This valley contains an incredible number of elephants and is probably one of the most prolific game areas in Africa. Unfortunately my pleasure in my appointment was undermined by the tragedy that led up to it. I was chosen to fill a vacancy caused by the death of an old campaigner, Charlie Ross. He had died, ironically, on the battlefield: 'Killed by his 350th elephant', as his epitaph in Mpika cemetery states with stark simplicity.

In those days all game services were performed by four Elephant Control Officers working under Provincial Commissioners in various provinces; there was no Game Department. Their main duty was to track down elephants invading native cultivation and to keep the settled areas free from their marauding. Charlie Ross, Freddy Hall, Harry Rangely and Captain Langham were the foundation members of this organisation, all experienced hunters of the old school and all first-class men. Alas, they are all dead now and with them went the last of the old pioneer elephant-hunters in Africa.

In fact, Charlie Ross was not the only one of this quartet to die in harness. Freddy Hall met a similar fate. But they, I think, would feel that they met their end in the way most true hunters would choose, had they to meet their Maker early. Were the two that survived any luckier, marking up their three-score years and ten and growing to depend more and more upon their memories of earlier exploits in the hunting field?

Fort Jameson used to be the Mecca of professional ivory hunters, and when I took up my appointment several of the old-time hunters were still in circulation. Most of them had been forced to give up hunting as a full-time occupation for, with the opening up of the country and the restriction on the number of elephant that could be shot on licence, they could no longer make a profitable living from their rifles. But they were still to be found throughout the country in the Bomas and out-stations like Fort Jameson, some of the luckier ones running wayside hotels or tobacco farms, the less adaptable serving in stores or doing subordinate jobs such as supervising labour gangs. Few of them could show any material reward for their life of adventure, like champion boxers shorn of their laurels. At one time these soldiers of fortune were untamed, unconventional and footloose wanderers, with all Africa as their battleground, but now they were subdued by advancing years and tied to a life of loneliness with nothing to live for but their thoughts. They had been too busy chasing adventure and trying to prove something to settle down and make a home. And now they were happy only if they could find an audience willing to listen to their reminiscences.

But they were colourful characters. The stories which circulate in Fort Jameson about their eccentricities are still part of the entertainment meted out to strangers who visit the town today. You can still hear about Ropesole Jones, a remittance man who, at the beginning of each quarter when his allowance was paid, would dress up in his immaculate white suit, with the inevitable rope-sole shoes, and, astride his donkey, would head a procession into town. His retinue was made up of his domestic staff, also dressed in spotless white uniforms – his head-boy following immediately behind the donkey, carrying a bottle of whisky, a tumbler and a soda syphon on a tray. After a week's glorious binge in the V.M.I. Club he would return home (perhaps not quite so immaculate) to await his next quarterly allowance. Then there was Champagne Charlie, Jereminsky, Hangman Smith and a host of others whose idiosyncrasies no doubt became more exaggerated with the passage of time.

Hangman Smith was never really a hunter and, like so many others, took up tobacco farming, although rather unsuccessfully. I do not know what qualifications apart from his versatility fitted him for the job but he was soon appointed official hangman at the local prison, receiving a remuneration of five pounds for each execution. He had a pathological hatred of missionaries and offered to hang as many as he could be provided with, at a reduced rate of fifteen shillings each. My only meeting with him occurred some years after this when he was an engine-driver of the goods train that travelled once or twice a week along the single-track railway line which runs from Blantyre and continues as two parallel streaks of rust disappearing into the distance, ending up Lord-knows-where on the shores of Lake Nyasa.

On this occasion I was with Bert Shultz, possibly the most imperturbable man I have ever met and certainly one of the most inveterate poachers. We were in a car together crossing the Nyasaland border after months away from civilisation when suddenly, miles from anywhere, we ran out of petrol. As usual in those days we carried our spare petrol in two four-gallon tins in a wooden case in the back of our box-body

Chevrolet. These tins and cases were the most valuable pieces
of domestic equipment in Africa and it seems a pity that such a
useful commodity should have gone out of fashion with the
advent of the petrol-filling station and the larger steel drum.
Every bush camp was fitted out with these boxes, made up
into tables, chairs, cupboards and shelves, and they were
exactly the right size for porters to carry. The tins made ideal
water buckets and when buried in a shallow trench provided
the camp with a perfect oven for baking bread. However, they
had one failing: when they were used for the purpose for which
they were designed they would sometimes leak, particularly
when bounced about in the back of a vanette over rough roads.
And this is exactly what had happened to us in this outlandish
spot.

We shrugged it off lightheartedly. Once used to touring in
Africa one assumes a fatalistic, resigned attitude towards
breakdowns of this, or almost any, sort. What did it matter
anyway? All around us stretched miles of inscrutable bush. We
were carrying enough provisions for several days and we could
always shoot something for the pot if necessary. So we brewed
ourselves some tea – an automatic procedure with any enforced
delay – and were relaxing over our third cup when a most
unusual sound made us sit up.

Impossibly, it seemed to come from a train in the near
distance. Bert and I looked at one another in amazement, for
neither of us had heard or seen such a thing for years. But sure
enough, a train it was. When it came into view the engine-
driver waved and his face lit up in recognition as he stopped his
engine.

Without realising it, we had run out of petrol only a few
yards from the single-track railway as it neared the shores of
Lake Nyasa. Hangman Smith, the driver, and Bert Shultz

were drinking friends of long standing, so it was a matter of seconds before he joined our tea-party and the two of them were exchanging gossip and reminiscing about the good old days in Fort Jameson. Behind him, his crew of four gazed on lugubriously.

With the subject practically exhausted, Smith suddenly looked up and asked why on earth we were camped in this Godforsaken spot. When he heard of our predicament he assured us that it could easily be remedied. He clambered back on to the footplate, put the train in reverse and returned to a siding fifteen miles back where he picked up a case of petrol for us.

It could only happen in Africa!

When I first arrived in Fort Jameson some of the tobacco planters still used to supplement their incomes by elephant-hunting. My appointment, therefore, was rather resented by the old-timers, who felt that if there was any hunting job to be done in their country one of them could do it more efficiently than a young whipper-snapper imported from Nyasaland. If successor there must be, why not, for instance, someone like Bert Shultz? However, I had little enough chance to feel the brunt of this antagonism as most of my time was spent in the bush and I came to town only for brief spells in order to buy supplies. When they saw that I tackled my job with enthusiasm, an exaggerated rumour began to circulate about my hunting prowess and the number of elephants I was shooting, so I was at last accepted into their guild by the old hunters and allowed by them to know something of my craft.

Before trying to explain how elephant control works, let me first describe the conditions that existed in the Luangwa Valley, where most of my hunting was done and where the villagers, whose welfare was our concern, eked out a rather precarious existence struggling against famine and the depredations of wild animals.

The Luangwa Valley is part of a geological formation known as the Great Rift Valley, which splits Africa in two from the Red Sea to South Africa. This continental fault consists of a chain of depressions which include, among other features, the Nile Valley and the Great Lakes of Central Africa. The Luangwa River runs through one of these valleys for almost four hundred miles until it joins up with the Zambezi, where the international borders of Zambia, Rhodesia and Portuguese territory all meet.

The Valley is almost two thousand feet lower than the surrounding plateau, and consequently much hotter. In the east there is no well-defined escarpment, but in the west there is an unbroken range extending for about two hundred miles. From the lip of this Muchingas escarpment you can look eastward across a sea of tree-tops two thousand feet below, and on a clear day with the sun at your back you can pick up the gleam of the Luangwa River more than forty miles away. Numerous small streams rush down the slopes during the rainy season and larger perennial rivers have cut deep scars through the escarpment on their journey from the plateau to the Luangwa River.

The rocks underlying the Valley floor are unlike any in this part of Africa (except those of the adjoining Zambezi valley). Geologists call these Karroo rocks and tell us they were formed more than one hundred million years ago under a large lake. The petrified remains of reptiles which lived at that time have been found in great profusion at Sitwe, in the north of the Valley. Fossilised trees are also very common, and I have seen some of these over forty feet long and four feet in diameter. Incidentally, I always had great difficulty in explaining to my men that these rocks were formed from living trees; invariably the answer would be: 'No, Bwana, these rocks are rocks.'

More recent inhabitants of the Valley have also left evidence of their stay – a Stone-Age hunter's axe from the Lukusuzi River; the pre-European metal hoe which was found at my camp at Mfuwe; the Portuguese cannon at Nawalya; the ruins of a colonist's farmhouse in the Mfushi River. I often wonder about the cannon and how it came to be abandoned at such a spot. Perhaps the Portuguese explorers who visited these parts three hundred years ago were dismayed at the prospect of hauling it up the Muchingas.

The vegetation changes as one descends from the wooded escarpment, with its great slabs of bare rock, and sets off for the river. At first the country is fairly flat, well wooded and quite similar to the plateau. This then gives way to scrubland with stunted trees on small very steep hills, which are usually carpeted with small quartz pebbles. In the dry season it is hot work walking over this type of country with its sparse shade, dry stream-courses and lack of game. As one approaches the river the ground becomes flatter and the mopane tree *(Colophospermum mopane)* becomes more common. This is the alluvial area of the Luangwa River. Mopane woodland, which predominates in this riverine area, varies enormously; in some sandy areas the trees are over sixty feet tall with a large straight bole; in clay areas the trees are much smaller and have a gnarled appearance. Tall mopane woodland is very like an English beech wood in appearance, as the undergrowth is sparse and it is always delightful walking country. Trekking through gnarled mopane, on the other hand, is much less pleasant; in the dry season the heavy black soil cracks extensively and it is rather like walking over frozen ploughed land, whereas in the rains one slithers and slides over black sticky clay.

The riverine area has many assorted habitats and during the dry season abounds with life. Picturesque lagoons, covered with bright green water-plants in a setting of giant shady trees, remind one of a stately English park. At a casual glance the impala and puku could easily be mistaken for red deer, but the illusion is immediately shattered when you see an elephant instead of a sheep, or a crocodile gliding stealthily across the surface of a lagoon where swans ought to be.

The Luangwa River twists and turns among the sand-channels down the centre of the Valley, providing its life-giving stream of fresh water. When the flow is reduced to a mere trickle at the height of the dry season and other streams and pools have given up their moisture to the thirsty tropical summer, the river attracts animals from far and wide and the area becomes a paradise for the nature-lover. Every stretch of river contains crocodiles basking on the sandbanks, which they share with sandpipers, white-headed plovers and dikkops (sometimes called a stone curlew, but the Afrikaans name of 'dikkop', meaning 'thick head', is far more descriptive).

Nearly every pool in which the water is deep enough for a hippo to submerge will support several of these grotesque animals, floating on the surface or standing partly submerged in the shallows, leaning their heads on one another's backs. They stumble into deep water at the first approach of danger. But it is the melancholy cry of the fish-eagle and the raucous honking of the Egyptian geese, rather than the sight of the more spectacular animals, which remain in my memory as typical of the unforgettable Luangwa, with its glorious wealth of fauna.

The rainy season, however, presents a completely different face. In November the cloudless summer skies give way to violent tropical storms; the tributaries, which are mere parched sandy river-beds in the dry season, come down in spate, carry-

With a mock charge an elephant shakes his head, demonstrates and trumpets before he starts. But with the real thing, below, he will curl his trunk and come without warning

A croc bit off half this calf elephant's trunk, but she survived for another year although she had to go down on her knees to graze

ing the run-off from the plateau country on either flank. The game disperses and the once-peaceful river appears in an entirely different guise – a turbulent, dark, muddy torrent raging down from bank to bank.

The river rarely floods its banks, but the alluvial area is flat and therefore usually waterlogged by the inflowing tributaries. Dense thickets occur in the riverine areas, and these are a favoured refuge for elephant and buffalo.

Large grassland areas, such as the inundated flats of the Kafue River, do not occur along the Luangwa River but perhaps in compensation there are two great plains on the west side of the Valley about midway between the escarpment and the Luangwa River. The Chifungwe and Lunda plains extend for about 120 square miles and are covered by tall kasense grass *(Setoria eylesii)*. This grows to about four feet during the rains and then remains during the dry season looking like what I always think of as 'standing hay'. Geologists, in their wisdom, say that these plains owe their formation to the type of underlying soil and rock. Elephants, in *their* wisdom, appear to regard the area as their private hayfield. Once, in August, I counted over seven hundred elephants browsing on the Chifungwe plain.

Elephant control operations take place during the rains and before the crops are harvested. The Valley is never completely submerged, and it is in the fertile pockets of soil above the flood-line that isolated groups of villages of the Asenga, Achewa and Akunda tribes scratch out a precarious living.

The main crop, in fact virtually their only crop, is millet, which is sometimes supplemented by rice, groundnuts, sweet potatoes or cow peas. The common form of agriculture is a shifting cultivation which entails hacking down and burning vast areas of trees so that the ash can fertilise the ground. When

c

after two or three years these lands are exhausted, the people move on and repeat the performance farther afield. It can be easily imagined how after a number of years these gardens become more and more widely flung until they are sometimes several miles away from the parent village.

When the scattered gardens become too remote the people select another site and rebuild the village. And so the process starts all over again. Of course it is just what the elephants want. For as the gardens are pushed out farther and farther into elephant terrain, easier and better conditions are created for them to raid in.

To guard against this, each family, which has its own garden, takes up residence in temporary huts near the crops while they are still growing, ready to drive off the predators. The huts are usually on high ant-mounds that give a commanding view over the field, or else are flimsy shelters built on stilts to give the necessary elevation overlooking the crops. During the day the piccanins and women drive off the birds and baboons. At night the men light fires, beat drums, shout and use various methods of alarm to drive off the elephant. Some beat a dried-out skin with a stick and this makes a resounding explosion which is a fair imitation of a rifle-shot and is most effective where elephants have learned to fear firearms.

The men keeping vigil in these gardens communicate with their neighbours by shouting when elephants are near by. On a clear night their shouts of alarm can be picked up several miles away and passed on to the next garden. In this way, the whole neighbourhood is alerted when danger approaches.

If a garden-owner fails to carry out these nightly precautions the consequences are disastrous. I have seen gardens, several acres in extent, completely devastated just because they were left unattended. Normally an elephant does not stay long in a garden if he is being shouted at and consequently the damage done is inconsiderable, but there are some elephants who completely lose their fear of man at night and go on feeding unperturbed in spite of all efforts to drive them off. Paradoxically, the same elephant, if tracked down, will make off in haste when he gets the first whiff of the hunter's scent.

My job, then, was elephant control: my area of operation this huge and intriguing Valley of the Luangwa.

4. *Elephant control*

The main purpose of my new job was to organise a system to control these marauding elephants in the Eastern Province of Northern Rhodesia (now Zambia). But how, one may ask with some justification, does one 'control' a large, unmanageable thing like an elephant? Surely it would not respond to disciplinary action in the same way as an unruly child?

In its present context *control* means to thin out the population by selective shooting or to drive elephants from an area where they are not wanted. The technique is to track down raiders as soon as possible after they have fed in the gardens and to shoot one or two from the group. This will deter the remainder from returning and drive them off to a more remote part of their range. It does not follow, of course, that it will prevent other groups raiding the same gardens or even the remainder of the punished herd raiding elsewhere, but if the operation is carried out systematically the accumulated effect is to reduce damage to a negligible proportion.

My tours in those days followed a regular pattern. I would camp in a central place from which I could cover as much ground as possible. Word would then be sent to outlying villages and gardens that the *Bwana wa Nyama* (a generic term for Game Rangers, or Government hunters, throughout Africa) was there and that in the event of elephants raiding a runner was to report to my camp early, before sun-up if possible. As reports were dealt with in strict rotation, the villagers needed little encouragement to dispatch such messages with the greatest alacrity. In fact, the potential reward of meat is one of the few incentives which can be guaranteed to convert their customary apathy into instant action.

I was always up an hour before dawn on the days I was to hunt. But, early as I was, I would inevitably find a villager already warming himself by the fire, waiting to tell me of the elephants which had raided his garden during the night. I well remember one chilly pre-dawn towards the end of the crop season in Chifunda's areas where raiding was particularly prevalent. As I sipped an early cup of tea I was as usual questioning a villager who had come into camp during the night.

He was a wizened, spindle-legged old man with a face like a walnut, from which a single canine tooth protruded when he smiled – which he did frequently. He was crouched over my camp fire with his hands practically in the flames, trying to get some warmth into his rheumaticky old bones. His name was Chuma though he could not have chosen a greater misnomer. For *Chuma* means 'wealth', and the few rags he wore did nothing to protect him against the chilly night air and belied any signs of material prosperity. But he was cheerful and happy, so perhaps *chuma* in the local dialect had a more liberal interpretation and did not necessarily refer to material wealth.

He had travelled several miles alone through the night, along bush paths with tall overhanging grass saturated with dew. It must have been an uncomfortable journey fraught with danger, for the spear he carried was not much protection against elephant or buffalo along his pitch-dark route. These discomforts were, I am sure, completely outweighed by his vision of a mountain of elephant meat, which he and his wives would enjoy for many months to come.

Chuma was a great actor. As I joined him over the fire he gave me a graphic account, emphasised by gesticulation and mime, of how he and his first wife had tried to drive off the elephants. He assured me that the leader of this group was the biggest and most voracious of all elephants in the Malambo (the local name for the Valley). He recognised the leader because of his broken tusk and told me he was a regular visitor to his garden, but this time he had brought his brothers with him. Between them they had finished up all his millet; not a single stalk was left standing. To emphasise this statement he brushed his palms one across the other and blew on them – a gesture of utter finality. Warrantable exaggeration, no doubt, but to prove his point he produced a stick about twenty inches long as the actual measurement of the elephant's footprint. For some reason this is considered irrefutable evidence and is commonly used by Africans in the Valley to support their claims of garden raiding. Although in the course of my work I often received false reports, mostly referring to visitations several days old, I would always rely on any report when a piece of stick had been produced as testimony.

It was still dark when our little party, led by Chuma, set off down the bush path. I had with me my gun-bearer and a carrier, with my scoff-box and blanket, for I always went prepared to stay out all day should the trail be particularly long. In the east the sky was a rosy pink as we arrived at Chuma's garden and there was just enough light to pick up the tracks of four bulls. I was not at all surprised to see a healthy crop of undamaged millet still standing. The elephants had trampled down a small patch in the north-east corner and made a passage through the centre of the garden, but the amount of damage relative to the whole was negligible.

The tracks strode off in a most purposeful manner, the

strides well spaced and the narrower hind foot over-stepping the more rounded fore-foot. The faster an elephant walks the farther the hind foot overlaps the fore-foot. When an elephant is striding out in this manner he digs his toes in and a little of the earth where he drags his fore-toe is scattered in front of each footprint. From these signs I concluded that they were probably travelling at about six miles an hour, so I had little chance of catching up with them until they slowed down to feed.

Their droppings also confirmed that they were going fast. For when an elephant really strides out, as these were doing, they do not stop to evacuate and their droppings are scattered as they fall on to and off their heels. You can learn a lot from an elephant's droppings while on the trail. According to the freshness of the dung you can tell how far ahead he is. And when it is warm to the back of your hand you can be sure he is not very far ahead. If the droppings occur frequently over a short distance you may reckon on his moving slowly. An elephant evacuates about every twenty minutes and this gives you a fair indication of his speed. The undigested grains of millet in their droppings were condemning enough evidence that these elephants were crop raiders. No further testimony was needed to convince me of their culpability.

Incidentally, an elephant's digestive system is most inefficient and this accounts for so much food passing through its body undigested. Recent experiments show that an elephant extracts only half the potential nourishment from the food it eats, which is probably the reason for its vast intake. Results of tests in East Africa show that an elephant's stomach contains 325 lb. of food and that it is completely evacuated every twelve hours – i.e. 650 lb. a day. On the other hand I have weighed more than 500 lb. dry weight in the stomach of a large bull in the Luangwa Valley.

Sometimes, when raiders are particularly confident that there will be no reprisals, they may after a night's foraging decide to sleep before the sun comes up. They usually do so on their feet but sometimes some will lie down. In this case the bull will find a suitable ant-hill and stretch out on his side. Elephants prefer to sleep on slightly sloping ground in order, I think, to be able to get to their feet more rapidly in case of alarm. The impression left by their body in the soft ground often shows the complete mould of one of the tusks and gives the hunter, if he is after ivory, a good idea of the size of his trophy. I have even occasionally come across them lying down, snoring their heads off. But they need very little sleep and most of their resting time is spent dozing on their feet. This is not surprising as they need sixteen to eighteen hours a day for feeding, which leaves little time for sleeping.

On this occasion I could see that my marauders had no intention of slowing down for some time. Only at midday did the tracks show that they had reduced speed, and about a mile farther on they had begun to feed. On coming to a desirable fodder tree they had scattered the leaves and branches around and trampled the ground flat. Their tracks now began to meander aimlessly and I could see where one elephant had stopped every now and again to tear down branches or dig for roots. This he did by swinging a front foot, pendulum-fashion, backwards and forwards, scooping the earth away and exposing a particularly succulent root, or rhizome, which had been located by his sensitive trunk.

But just as I felt confident that we were coming up to them the spoor joined up with the tracks of a cow herd. This might be tricky; if the party of bulls decided to remain with the cows our chances of sorting them out in such thick cover would be poor. If on the other hand it was just a temporary overlapping of the tracks, then there was a fair chance we could unravel the bull tracks, although this is always a tedious business and demands a certain amount of tracking skill.

The sun was now well overhead and the wind, as often happens at this time of day, was fitful and for ever changing its course. It kept eddying round in circles – not the most favourable conditions for becoming involved with a breeding cow herd.

The occasional bull tracks showed up unmistakably overlaying the cow spoor and the diminutive prints of the calves, but our progress was now very slow. Sometimes it was impossible to separate the tracks, so we had to follow in the wake of the cow herd, checking carefully to see that none of the bull tracks went off to the side. It was not long before we heard the breaking of branches in front of us, then a high-pitched squeal which told us that the cows were ahead.

The shrill squeals which accompany a cow herd when it is supposed to be resting is an unnerving sound when heard at close quarters. But it goes on all the time as militant mothers and irascible aunts for ever try to maintain discipline among an incredible number of calves and adolescents. Bulls rarely advertise their presence in such a manner. But what about the bulls? Did we have to get mixed up with that lot in front of us in order to find them? My gun-bearer and tracker seemed to lack their earlier determination and Chuma was hanging back, frankly worried. Meat to him was the most valuable commodity in the world but the urge for self-preservation seemed to have an atrophying effect on his usually insatiable appetite. Obviously none of them was keen to go on, but I had no intention of giving up; so we pressed on regardless, slowly picking out the larger bull spoor from the main herd.

The ultimate test of a good elephant tracker is to be able to unravel a criss-cross spoor. In damp ground this is easy enough but all one's skill is required to follow it over dry ground, for an elephant treads very softly in spite of its bulk and its large spongy feet leave little impression on dry grass. Buffalo or eland or any of the larger cloven-hoofed animals are easier to track because their sharp hooves cut into the hard earth. One's greatest difficulty is when tracks are laid down over successive days. After a mile or so of painstaking unravelling you find that the tracks you are following are stale. Then you have to back-track and pick them up again where you last saw an indisputably fresh mark. It is here that the way a blade of grass or a bruised leaf lies can save you hours of tracking. A piece of grass which has been taken along in the wake of an animal will spring back into position against an upstanding stalk and remain on the side that your quarry is travelling; if it ends up on the other side then the indications are that the animal is going the other way. Just a very small clue like this, added to other signs which only the trained eye would discern, can tell you what you want to know. Luckily my tracker on this occasion was an expert and between us we managed to keep on the right spoor.

With the cow herd only three or four hundred yards ahead we picked out one of the bulls' tracks peeling off to one flank. Cautiously we followed this and to our great relief found that it veered off away from the route the cows had taken. We continued for another hour or so before we came up to the bulls in very thick cover where visibility was not more than ten to fifteen yards. We could hear them feeding a hundred yards ahead but because of the poor visibility we had little chance of spotting them until we were much closer. We made a slight detour to give ourselves a more favourable wind and now, disregarding the spoor and relying on our sight and hearing, we crept forward slowly – a few yards at a time, waiting, straining our ears and eyes for the elephants to indicate their positions.

The sound of a branch being torn down told us that one of the bulls was feeding some distance away to our left, but I wanted to place each animal before manœuvring into a shooting position. We concentrated like this for several minutes, hardly daring to breathe, all our senses tingling. I was hoping the wind would not change and give them our scent and send them crashing off, bulldozing all the small saplings in their path and leaving us ignorant of the direction from which they would come.

I was watching the faces of my boys, mask-like and tense. Suddenly the gun-bearer nodded and with his eyes gestured to our right. I could only just hear a faint swishing noise of branches being parted but this seemed to me even farther away than the first one we had pinpointed. Then, about seventy yards ahead, we saw the top of a small tree moving. This indicated the third elephant; there was still one to place. We remained in a keyed-up state, waiting to locate him.

After what seemed an age I decided not to wait any longer, since I felt sure we would have heard the missing elephant had he been immediately in front of us. I waited for my three attendants to climb into the comparative safety of a large tree and then crept forward towards the place where the branches had moved. As the distance shortened, I could hear those almost imperceptible faint noises of a very large unseen animal ahead. I saw part of him, a darker patch of grey among the dense bush. It could have been any part of his anatomy. I advanced another ten yards, slightly into wind to get a clearer view of his head and shoulders which were facing three-quarters on to me and offered a reasonable brain shot. I took a deep breath. I could afford to hesitate no longer in case he got my wind. I fired and he dropped instantaneously. He had no idea what struck him. I could hear the rest of the herd crashing off through the trees and I gave my boys the 'all-clear' for them to come back to earth.

Chuma's grinning face, with his prominent canine sticking out like the prow of a ship, is a picture I shall always remember. This was his day. The boys' exuberance was in direct contrast to the subdued, apprehensive silence of the past few hours and they manifested this release from tension first by solemnly shaking hands with one another and then by rather boisterously thumping one another on the back. After brewing the inevitable cup of tea on the site we trekked back to camp, arriving with the lengthening shadows of the late afternoon.

When an elephant has been shot it is usual to call up the headman of the local village for a briefing on the distribution of the meat and the safe custody of the tusks, which had to be carried to the nearest Government depot. I had no need to call in the headman of Chuma's village: he had been waiting in camp all afternoon, anticipating the welcome news.

The following day the entire community would go to the dead elephant in one straggling, vociferous column and tackle the great hulk with knives and hatchets. The pandemonium from this uncontrolled mass of shrieking men and women, some of them standing knee-deep inside the disembowelled beast, all squabbling for possession of the choicest cuts with their arms and bodies bespattered with blood and offal, is a sight to see only once in a lifetime. Their uninhibited greed, together with the stench of the sweating hysterical bodies steeped in offal, is a most nauseating experience. I left most of the business to the headman to supervise the following day, while I packed my camp and moved on to the next Chief's area.

Touring in the Luangwa Valley in the rainy season is not an easy matter. Fortunately I had no set schedule, so time was unimportant. There was no means of transport between one group of settlements and another except on foot, and when the rivers were in full spate this was sometimes a hazardous undertaking. Occasionally, uprooted trees and other debris would be swept down in the racing current and a river-crossing could sometimes involve several days' wait until the water had subsided sufficiently to allow one's party to swim or wade over.

Among my regular gang of about twenty carriers I had one boy who was my 'official river-tester'. His name was Long-one and he stood about six foot four inches and was as thin as a bean-pole. He was an untiring and cheerful worker and took great pride in his specialised status. Whenever there was a flooded river to cross Long-one would wade in and, if he could walk on the bottom with his up-stretched hands showing above the water, then we considered it safe to attempt the crossing. This was the criterion accepted quite cheerfully by the remainder of the porters. If the test showed that the river was too deep we would camp on the bank until the flood receded. When we crossed most of the loads were carried on out-stretched arms above the head, while the men walked on the bottom, sometimes with their heads completely submerged. Why they were not swept away by the current always puzzled me. Perhaps the loads helped to keep their feet on the ground. I personally rarely succeeded in walking against the current and usually had to swim across diagonally, ending up a hundred yards or so downstream. Any special load to be kept dry, such as flour, sugar, mealie meal or my ammunition, would be wrapped in a tarpaulin and my best swimmer would ferry these loads across in a tin bath.

A full-scale river-crossing operation would take a whole morning or afternoon and was always carried out in the most competitive and joyful spirit. The more timid carriers, who usually put off their ordeal until all the others had crossed, came in for considerable ridicule and ribald jests from the more experienced men. The greatest joke of all was when one of the porters lost his footing and was swept away in the flood. This never failed to raise a burst of riotous laughter. The load would invariably be recovered by one of the onlookers as it was being swept downstream. When all the loads were across we would dry out, have a meal and reorganise for the next phase of our journey.

These were cheerful, carefree people. Their needs were few and they were happy provided I could keep their bellies full, which presented no difficulty because of the surfeit of elephant meat available to them.

In those days it seemed to me that hunting elephants was the most exciting, exhilarating pursuit in the world. One had to be in the pink of condition to stand the pace, travelling from sun-up to sun-down for weeks on end under the most arduous conditions. To catch up with the typical garden raider you must be prepared to journey over swampy ground, through impenetrable thickets and tall grass where the visibility is no more than an arm's length. Early in the morning the nine foot high elephant grass is saturated with dew and you become wetter and colder as the journey proceeds until the sun is high enough to dry you out. Then the humidity becomes stifling and bayonet-like grass seeds work their way through your clothing until you think you have reached the ultimate in discomfort: but not at all, for you have yet to meet the buffalo bean, an instrument of torture devised by the devil himself. These beans grow on thin, spiralling tendrils which climb up the tall grass stems and, as you brush past, the velvet-like bean showers down minute poisonous hairs which get into your clothes and down your neck, driving you frantic with irritation. The more you scratch, the worse it becomes.

The hardships and privations, however, are soon forgotten in the thrill of the chase. The memory of all these discomforts vanishes when the spoor is fresh and at every step you expect to hear a tell-tale crack as an elephant ahead tears down a branch, or the flop of ears as he flaps them in an effort to keep cool or drive off the insects. Perhaps the first indication that your quarry is ahead is the deep rumbling noise which sounds like distant thunder, as his digestive system attempts to cope with his enormous intake. This build-up to the climax is the most exciting part of the hunt and at that stage in my career seemed to be the most thrilling experience on earth.

I shot more than two hundred elephants that season. It was dangerous work but I felt I had to take up a challenge so as to prove to myself that I was tough and unafraid. The fact that I was simultaneously performing a duty which I convinced myself was important and beneficial to the community encouraged me to rationalise this rather immature compulsion. Besides, I was drawing nearer to my original heroes. I was practically a hero myself!

5. In search of sanctuary

After a full season hunting elephants I began to feel that the emphasis should be changed, that we should not rely entirely on crop protection (which resulted in so many elephants being killed) but also upon more determined efforts to drive the elephants into sanctuaries. In such a vast, sparsely settled area, surely there was ample room for both the human and the elephant population to survive, provided that the elephants were taught to behave.

An elephant is by nature a peace-loving creature and able to adapt itself to new conditions far more easily than any other animal. So in theory, if enough large sanctuaries were set aside where the elephants could remain unmolested they would soon learn to treat such areas as their homes and thus have little excuse for entering and damaging the settled areas. Unfortunately elephants are not theorists, and garden-raiding elephants in particular quickly acquire a taste for cultivated crops and teach the younger bulls to follow suit.

But though all bulls are potential raiders, they have not all acquired the raiding habit. Prevention, as always, is better than cure, especially as cow elephants are much shyer of humans and do not normally raid gardens at all. On the whole, the arguments in favour of sanctuary were strong.

My next task, therefore was to select suitable sanctuary areas where the elephants could feel inviolate, and then to recruit and train sufficient hunters to deal summarily with the offenders in the settled areas. First of all, I realised I would have to train at least a dozen more elephant hunters. It was better to use a village hunter brought up in the lore of the bush, train him to use a modern rifle and instil some discipline into him, rather than try to teach an intelligent, sophisticated ex-askari type the rudiments of bushcraft. A true elephant hunter is born and cannot really be trained, so it was my job to try to find ready-made material and convert it to my requirements.

My first batch of trainees went through an intensive military-type weapon training course, which included sufficient drill to smarten them up and oft-repeated lectures on game laws and elementary conservation principles. When it came to target practice, I would start them off with a small ·22 rifle to avoid the punishing recoil of the heavy elephant rifle which is inclined to make a person flinch and pull off the target. For if I had taught a recruit to use the heavy rifle from the beginning he would invariably have become gun-shy and no amount of subsequent training would have cured him. By this method, when the recruits eventually graduated on to a ·404 rifle many of them became excellent marksmen. Once trained and qualified they could then be put to understudy one of the more experienced elephant hunters for a whole season.

When I found myself in an area where one of my apprentice hunters was stationed, I would take him out and watch him perform. When he had shot his elephant we would hold a post-mortem to discuss the bullet penetration and the vital shot. Later, when the animal was cut up, we would examine the position of the vital organs.

One of my main difficulties was to find someone reliable enough to carry out instructions and not abuse his authority once he was miles away from supervision. By the very nature of their calling, these hunters were individualists with strong personalities and a built-in resistance to authority. A 'fundi', as he was called, with tons of meat at his disposal became the most popular and influential man in his community and could demand practically anything he wanted from the people. His grain bins were always full, even in the lean years, and he could claim as many wives as he wished. This power could be abused. The hunters were in danger of having their heads turned and I would often find my own ones seriously undermining the traditional authority of the Chief.

How I 'recruited', or more correctly 'press-ganged', one of my best fundis into the ranks of our control staff illustrates to what limits I was prepared to go in order to get the right man. Kalamadoda, the village hunter, was a fascinating, ugly, gangling native who walked with his toes turned in at such an angle as to give an alarming impression of deformity. His light brown skin proclaimed a mixture of Arab blood which doubt-less his ancestors had inherited from the slave-trading days. But he was incurably optimistic, a cheerful, light-hearted rogue.

He was also a notorious poacher and already had two con-victions to his name. He knew the Valley round the Lukusuzi River like the back of his hand, for he spent practically every day sloping through the bush, hunting with his antique muzzle-loading gun, shooting anything he could find and trad-ing the meat for grain and other more personal favours. No other hunter knew as much as he did about the ways of animals in the bush. On one occasion he shot ten buffalo in one day with his muzzle-loading gun, and anyone who has seen a muzzle-loader operate will appreciate what a feat this is, for there is no time to reload and take a second shot before the herd stampedes. These guns have no backsight and, to aim, the hunter merely points the barrel in the general direction of the animal at point-blank range, pulls the trigger, counts several seconds and, with eyes tightly closed, awaits the explosion. There is usually just enough time between pulling the trigger and the resulting explosion to offer up a short prayer to the guardian spirit responsible for the safety of all hunters. Even then, reloading after each shot is a finicky business. One has to make sure of each shot and then start the hunt all over again after claiming each victim.

There was no doubt that Kalamadoda would be more useful on my staff where I would have some sort of control over him, rather than on his own as an indiscriminate poacher. Besides, I rather liked him. There was certainly no misunderstanding between us. Every time I saw him I told him in no uncertain terms that I would catch him for poaching and that next time he would be sent to prison. He would reply with a grin from ear to ear: 'All right, Bwana, but you've got to catch me first!' We had a mutual respect for, and friendship towards, each other and whenever I hunted near his village he would attach himself to my party as a gun-bearer and guide. I have never met anyone who could unravel a difficult spoor as well as Kalamadoda. He was a born hunter and I needed him on my staff. I set about obtaining him.

It took me several months to build up the evidence I needed. By posting an informer at Kalamadoda's village I was able to secure enough evidence to charge him on twelve counts for contravening the game laws. When the case was heard before the Magistrates' Court I gave evidence and asked for his game licence to be removed and his gun to be confiscated. After the hearing I paid Kalamadoda's fine personally. Later, when he came to see me in my office, he bore me no malice but was as friendly as ever. When I asked him if he wanted a job on my staff he replied: 'Of course, Bwana, I thought that was the arrangement. You have drawn my teeth – what else can I do?'

I shall never forget taking him out for the first time to see how he would shape in front of elephants after he had gone through his preliminary training. We picked up the spoor of a small group of bulls in the garden of Manga's village in Kazembe's country near the foothills of the eastern escarpment. After tracking these elephants for several hours we came up to them in fairly open woodland in the foothills.

Circling downwind we halted about fifty yards from two of the bulls who were feeding not more than fifteen yards apart. I beckoned to Kalamadoda, gesturing him to shoot the larger of the two bulls but not to shoot more than one. For all the concern he showed you might have thought I had asked him to go and fetch me some water. He sauntered casually forward, his rifle still at the trail, his toes turning in even more than usual. Strolling up between the two elephants, without any attempt to put his rifle at the 'ready', he turned his back on the small elephant and looked at me for confirmation before raising his rifle at the larger one.

Receiving it, he gave the bull a broadside from about five yards. Then, without any thought for his victim, he turned his back on the huge tottering animal and in a conversational manner pointed to the smaller bull which had slewed round in surprise with his ears out menacingly, and requested permission to shoot it. Kalamadoda hated the thought of seeing five or six tons of meat move off unharmed.

Meanwhile, behind him the first elephant, although staggering and fatally wounded, was still capable of doing considerable damage. I screamed at him to finish off the elephant he had shot, and called him a very rude name as I kept my rifle at my shoulder ready to put a shot into whichever elephant decided to kill him.

My intervention was not necessary. The first elephant suddenly collapsed. Its companion moved its head as if it had had second thoughts about attacking and lumbered angrily and ineffectively away.

Kalamadoda was not brave: he was fearless and foolhardy and treated all dangerous animals with contempt. I did not predict a very long future for him, but I was wrong. He was sacked ten years later by my successor for repeated and flagrant disobedience. For he was a killer and could not be made to see the purpose of shooting a limited number of elephant when with little additional effort he could shoot the whole lot. He was quite incorrigible and totally undisciplined. But for a while he served his purpose well.

Perhaps also he provides a good moment to consider the moral justification for elephant control, although he himself was hardly a good argument for it.

It has always been a subject of controversy. The ardent preservationist, for instance, is appalled at the wastage of animal life involved as a punishment for stealing what virtually amounts to a few bags of corn. And if the only considerations were economic his argument would be sound, provided a system could be organised for compensating the garden owner in kind for his loss of grain. But owing to the difficulty of communication among these scattered villages during the rainy season, such compensation would be well-nigh impossible. The whole existence of these primitive people depends upon their cultivation of crops. Tsetse fly exclude the possibility of herding stock for meat and so grain is virtually their only means of sustenance. It must be realised, too, that these villagers are quite cut off from normal centres of supply and totally lack the advantages of urban dwellers who can earn money and buy their requirements from the shop at the corner of the street whenever they like.

But let me disillusion any reader who thinks that elephants are being exterminated merely in the name of 'control'. In spite of the heavy toll each year in the Luangwa Valley, which probably holds 75 per cent of the territory's population, the elephant is steadily *increasing*. The present population is considered by some to be nearly three times that of forty years ago. And one of the main factors responsible for the increase is elephant control. This may seem rather paradoxical but it must be remembered that all elephants shot on control operations or by sportsmen with licences are males. The breeding herds are therefore not reduced. In fact this culling process has the effect of improving the breeding stock by thinning out the surplus bulls, and is the normal technique followed by most cattle ranchers.

This is not my final word on the increasing population of elephants, nor on the implications of severe over-population. I will refer to these in a later chapter.

CHANGE OF ENVIRONMENT

6. War clouds

On the third of September 1939, I was on patrol in Kambwiri's country in the Luangwa Valley. News of the outbreak of war did not reach me until nearly two weeks later.

It was presented to me in a typical 'cleft stick' by a District Messenger sent out by the District Commissioner in Lundazi. As I was still on the strength of the King's African Rifles Reserve in Nyasaland, I was misguided enough to think that my services were urgently required to defend the Empire. Without further thought and in spite of the fact that I had already done a long patrol that day, starting at dawn and arriving at Msekeni's village after noon, where the D.C.'s Messenger caught up with me, I packed a haversack and prepared to trek up to Lundazi, nearly eighty miles away, where I had left my motor vehicle a month ago.

The preparations I made before leaving were of necessity hurried, but I left the camp in care of my *capitao*, a very reliable Yao from Nyasaland. I also gave him instructions to pack up and follow me into the Boma at his own pace.

So began one of the longest walks I have ever undertaken. With one of my best carriers as a pace-setter we started off walking continuously through the night and arrived at Lundazi Boma at noon the next day. Taking into account the twenty miles I had covered before Msekenis, I must have accomplished a hundred mile trek in just over thirty hours. I have never before or since slept on my feet, but during that journey I found that for mile after weary mile I walked automatically in a subconscious daze, with no recollection of time or space.

I need not have troubled. It was an entirely wasted journey. For when I eventually reported to the Provincial Commissioner in Fort Jameson, I learned to my sorrow that I was not required for the moment and should return to work and await normal instructions; if I were needed I would be called up, like everyone else, through the usual channels.

Despite the telegrams I sent to military headquarters hoping to by-pass these orders, I could not persuade anyone that my services were sufficiently important for the War Office to call me up at once. One thing about living on your own in the bush for months on end is that you are in no doubt about your own importance. It is surprising, therefore, and rather irritating to find that others also have their problems which take no account of yours. It is also rather salutary.

While I waited hopefully in Fort Jameson for the verdict, the Provincial Commissioner, Mr. Brooks, more commonly known as 'Bertie the Bwana', invited me to a sundowner party at the Residency. It was for the following evening and, though I did not know it at the time, was to be one of the most unorthodox parties ever given there.

In those days, of course, it was customary for the King's representative in the province to hold such parties periodically, and all officials and local dignitaries were invited and expected to attend. As it happened I only had my bush clothes with me, yet I had no option but to accept. Borrowing something more suitable and only too aware that I was in somebody else's clothes, I arrived at the Residency a little after schedule.

Immediately I sensed that something besides myself was wrong. Instead of the usual smooth routine of drinks and sandwiches handed round by well-trained African servants, I noticed that several of the guests were undertaking these unaccustomed duties themselves. They moved oddly, with a stiff self-conscious amateurishness as if in a cheap cafetaria. Sidling over to the corner of the room for a quick drink, I learnt the reason for this strange domestic crisis.

As a wartime precaution all communities – no doubt throughout the Empire – had been instructed by the War Office to draw up a suitable plan in the event of an unexpected air attack. All citizens were to be told what to do should such an emergency occur. From the Provincial Commissioner's office in Fort Jameson a circular had emanated to all householders under the heading: 'In the event of enemy attack from the air.' It went on to explain what precautions were to be taken should the Luftwaffe decide to make a strategic attack on Fort Jameson. All personnel should evacuate the buildings immediately and take to the bush until enemy activity ceased. Householders were to ensure that all their domestic servants were conversant with the terms of the circular. All recipients were to acknowledge its receipt and confirm that appropriate action had been taken.

In those days George Hardy was the manager of Mandala Stores, our local (and only) department store; he was also, as it happened, part-time superintendent of the airport, which was sited eight miles out of town. Each week the Rapide aircraft, which came in every Tuesday, would swoop down over Mandala and alert George, who would automatically take off along the dusty road to the airport in his vanette and collect the passengers or cargo, and also brew tea for the pilot.

On this particular Tuesday all the domestic staff in town had been meticulously briefed by their Bwanas what to do should an 'ndege' (aeroplane) attack them: they were to take to the bush until further notice. It was then, as the Rapide swept low over Mandala to alert George, that with one accord the entire domestic staff in Fort Jameson took to the woods, among them the servants from the Residency.

They did not stay there long, at least not all of them. Most continued through the trees to their homes and villages. It was several weeks before they started trickling back to work and life returned to normal.

This was probably the worst war casualty suffered by the town during the six years of hostilities. It was certainly, in retrospect, the most amusing.

7. Outpost of empire

At least eight months later, when I was on tour on the Congo–Tanganyika border, I at last received my calling-up papers, this time 'through the usual channels' via the District Commissioner at Mporokoso. But before this happened I had been posted to the Northern Province away from my beloved Valley.

Rather than travel south by car, then westwards to Lusaka and northwards to Mpika and my destination, I decided to take a short cut and trek due west with my carriers towards Mpika. This direct route is only two hundred miles, compared with more than four times that distance by road. My possessions were few in those days and as always went about with me on the heads of my porters, so I was delighted to have this opportunity to explore an unknown part of the Valley and to climb the wall of the Muchingas escarpment. Hitherto I had known it only as a fascinating purple mountain range, forming the western barrier of the Valley behind which I had so often watched the sun go down.

I started off with twenty-two carriers and arrived at Mpika ten days later. Mpika Boma was typical of many administrative outposts found throughout Central Africa where a small body of dedicated men attempted to uphold the traditions of a once-extensive Empire. My first impression, as I trekked into the Boma with my carriers, was of a picturesque collection of

59

half a dozen redbrick houses nestling in the surrounding hills. Each house consisted of four or five rooms in a row, enclosed by a wide mosquito-gauzed veranda. The dim interior was relieved by very high ceilings, with fanlights above the level of the lean-to veranda. There was not much originality in the design and the same house could be found repeated in any out-station one visited. For in those days the D.C. was his own building contractor and had to burn his own bricks; hence simplicity was the order of the day. Besides, these houses had one great advantage: they were cool and airy.

When I arrived at the D.C.'s house to introduce myself to Douglas and his wife, Rachel, it was pouring with rain. I knocked at the veranda door and was rather surprised to be met by a tall, gangling man I took to be a P.W.D. motor mechanic. He wore a dirty pair of overalls, had smears of oil across his face and was up to his armpits in grease. I thought it strange that he should appear in the D.C.'s house in that condition but supposed he had been invited in to take shelter from the rain. His first words served to confirm his artisan status. 'Do you happen to know the firing order for a Morris Cowley?' he asked rather anxiously.

'No,' I said, 'I'm afraid I don't.' I went on, more abruptly than I meant, to ask if I could see the D.C.

'Yes,' he said smiling, 'you can. I am the D.C.'

I introduced myself formally and when he had wiped most of the grease from his hands on to the back of his overalls, we gingerly shook hands.

'Rachel!' he shouted across the veranda. 'Mr. Carr has arrived.'

To my amazement Rachel appeared from the sitting-room behind in an even greasier state.

'I'm afraid we're in a bit of a muddle,' she said with what seemed to me then considerable understatement. I could see exactly what she meant. For as I stepped into it, the sitting-room bore no resemblance whatever to any normal room in a house. It was more like a garage workshop. In the middle lay the disembowelled engine of a motor-car (I presume the Morris Cowley, whose firing order I had been requested to diagnose), with the cylinder-head off. The mantelshelf and bookcases were liberally littered with piston heads and other engine parts. The carpet was protected with sheets of newspaper (two-month-old copies of the London *Times*) on which were spread out, in total disarray, a confusion of nuts, bolts, piston-rings and other vital parts presumably, in spite of their chaotic appearance, in some special order of dismantling.

They had decided, they explained, to give the car a complete overhaul during the week-end. And the only place suitable or dry enough for such work was the house. They had started, reasonably enough, on the veranda but the driving rain had moved them on into the sitting-room. Rachel is the only woman I have ever come across capable of retiming an engine and setting the points of a distributor.

As it turned out they were two of the most charming and hospitable hosts imaginable and, in fact, typical of many of the Colonial administrators I met on my travels among the out-stations in Northern Rhodesia. Typical, that is, in their spon-taneous kindness, but no one could accuse them of being typical in their behaviour.

Although normally I prefer to remain independent and camp on my own when paying official visits to Bomas, they were so genuinely insistent that I should take over the guest-house that I gratefully accepted their offer. Since I had been on the move continuously during the past few weeks through heavy rain-storms I had had little chance to dry out my bedding, which was now not only damp but thick with mildew. It would be wonderful to relax and experience the luxury of a well-aired bed once more.

That evening to my surprise and, it must be admitted, my relief we dined in great contrast to our initial meeting at a beautifully laid table with candlelight glimmering from a heavy silver candelabrum which had graced the table of many of Douglas's ancestors. A soft-footed servant in flowing white gown and red embroidered waistcoat served us unobtrusively and well, his face merging with the shadows except when the light from the candles caught it as he bent forward to refill our glasses with the delicious and aptly chosen wine. If I had been a potentate, dining at Government House, I could not have been more lavishly entertained.

My hostess, however, still lapsed occasionally into one of her delightfully inimitable moments of eccentricity. Earlier that evening, while Douglas and I were having drinks, she appeared in a gorgeous outfit which might have been, and almost certainly was, modelled exclusively for her. It was in stirring contrast to her mechanic's suit of the afternoon and I watched her with admiration. Douglas, however, as he handed her a drink murmured in a not altogether inaudible aside, 'Rachel, dear, your shoes.'

It was only then that I noticed her stockinged feet.

'I know, darling, I couldn't find them,' she replied repentently. 'I suppose I must have put them somewhere.'

With a resignation born of constant habit Douglas went to look for the missing footwear. I heard him scrummaging in the bedroom and was not wholly surprised when he returned empty-handed.

'What were you doing just before going to change?' he asked, with patient but penetrating acumen.

'Oh, of course, sorting out the drink cupboard,' she replied.

With considerably more spring in his step Douglas strode across to the drinks cupboard and opened the door. There, wedged between a bottle of French Vermouth and another of Drambuie, were the missing shoes.

I sank back bemused, in a coma of good food and drink. Their voices seemed to come at me from a great distance. Even so I found it hard to believe my ears when I heard Rachel casually addressing the waiter as Crankshaft.

I sat up, my mind boggling. Was it possible that everyone in this house was called after the parts of a motor-car? Was their interest in the internal combustion engine as simple as it first appeared? Was there perhaps a note of fetishism, even, not to put too fine a point on it, of hysteria in their concern?

I stirred uneasily, then shrugged it off. After all, what business was it of mine? Why not lie back and savour the pleasures of this *Toad of Toad Hall* world? What, I wondered, would my own nickname be if I were to become a member of the household? My surname already qualified for a place in their household but what prefix would they add? With somewhat heavy humour I leant forward to inquire.

They looked at me blankly. No, they assured me, it was not like that at all. Crankshaft did not owe his name to them. It had nothing to do with their personal preoccupation with things mechanical. That was purely coincidental.

Yes, it was quite true; to them the fact seemed clearly less extraordinary than it did to me that all the members of the household bore the names of spare parts. But the reason lay elsewhere – with a predecessor in fact. To me their explanation was no less strange.

Apparently, when he retired many years ago the former D.C. had pensioned off his head servant, who happened to be

Crankshaft's father, amid mutual expressions of goodwill and regret. Crankshaft's father duly left for his native village, carrying with him the affection of the family and the D.C.'s old discarded motor car manual.

In those days a book really was a book, even if no one could read it. It brought with it an aura of mystery and promise. It imposed status especially if, as in this case, it was the only book in the village.

In Crankshaft's father's village it was both a link with the past and a promise of the future. It achieved a position of eminence. And, from time to time, when itinerant mission boys passed by on their travels they would be only too delighted to demonstrate their newly acquired skill by reading aloud from the book. They rolled out the references joyously, intoning the instructions and rejoicing in the exotic nomenclature. Children, as well as grown-ups, listened entranced. Later, when the time for the ceremony of choosing their adult names arrived (it was the custom in those parts for the children to choose the names they would go by for the rest of their lives when they reached a certain age), they plumped for those from the book. It must have puzzled many a subsequent D.C. who came on tour to check the village census to find there such names as Halfshaft, Crownwheel, Axle, and Radiator.

The next morning I paid off my carriers and arranged to take on a relief team from the local Awemba tribe. After that I spent a very happy three days with my unconventional host and hostess. In those days a District Commissioner had to play many parts. He had to be road engineer, building contractor, medical practitioner, agriculturist, tax-collector and veterinary officer. In fact he was responsible for all the Government services and could only rely on an occasional visit from technical officers for advice. Above all, he was the magistrate and upholder of the law. According to your state of health, you could either be married or buried by him.

At that time, since his assistant had been called up for war service, Douglas was the only official in a district twice the size of the largest county in England. He had to have a passing knowledge of all these trades, apart from being the father confessor and adviser to a large indigenous population.

I have come across Douglas many times in subsequent years as he ascended the hierarchy of the Colonial Service – first as a Provincial Commissioner in Fort Jameson, then as a Permanent Secretary in Lusaka, the capital and ending up as Governor of Somaliland. But the further he advanced the more nostalgic I know he felt about his early life as a D.C. in an out-station where resourcefulness and improvisation were his chief weapons and which he administered alone with paternal tolerance.

The last morning of my visit I accompanied him on a tour of inspection. We had looked over the Boma, ending with the dispensary, when I noticed across the yard a queue of African women carrying laden baskets, the contents of which were being weighed by a District Messenger and then dumped unceremoniously on to a growing pile on a native mat spread on the floor.

Before handing the basket back to the owner, the Messenger would laboriously write a few figures on a piece of paper and hand it to the woman. Every now and again the routine would be interrupted whilst a mother attended to the howling demands of a baby slung on her back. She would simply pull the sling containing the protesting infant to her front, uncover a pendulant breast and stuff it into the eagerly waiting mouth. Immediately the crying would stop. With equal sang-froid she would then collect her piece of paper from the Messenger and proceed to another queue which was forming at another table.

Here sat an African clerk, resplendent in his white uniform, issuing what I discovered to be tax receipts. The atmosphere of a market prevailed and there was incessant haranguing between the Messenger and the women bringing in their wares. The noise was indescribable.

What were they doing? It looked intriguing, and I wandered across to see what it was all about. The ever-increasing pile of produce mounting up in front of the District Messenger fascinated me. I prodded it cautiously and found it to consist of black shrivelled-up objects about the size and shape of one's little finger. I knew at once what these were: dried-out caterpillars, of course.

Caterpillars are a greatly sought-after delicacy among these tribes. At a particular season of the year a large grey-green caterpillar which is known as 'matondo' swarms in profusion on a specific tree in the open woodlands (*Julbernadia paniculata*). There, and only on this particular tree, the moths lay their eggs and when they hatch months later the caterpillars feed exclusively on this particular foliage. These caterpillars swarm in profusion at a certain time of year and it is uncanny to walk through a woodland supporting *Julbernadia paniculata* and find several acres of them completely denuded of every vestige of foliage, standing stark and bare against the skyline whilst other species are in full leaf.

When the caterpillars swarm, the villagers go out in a party and collect them in baskets. It was this that they had just done. Their method is very destructive, for they usually chop the trees down, finding it easier than climbing up on improvised ladders. There are hundreds of thousands of trees, so why should anyone bother about conserving them? Their attitude towards trees is very reminiscent of Kalamododa's attitude towards elephants. After a caterpillar-collecting party has taken away its crop the woodland looks as if a hurricane has passed by, with trees lain waste in all directions.

As these caterpillars form a rich protein diet they are in great demand. The head is broken off and a dark green, slimy jelly is squeezed out and discarded. It is the fleshy outer skin which is laid out in the sun to dry and ultimately eaten. I cannot say I am partial to caterpillars: they taste rather like rubbery, flavourless shrimps. But I suppose it is all right if you close your eyes and cease to think about what you are eating.

Anyway, in the Mpika Boma they were in great demand as rations. Douglas must have been grateful for any type of protein which would help to fortify the poor nutritional value of maize meal which he was forced to feed to the large numbers of labourers, prisoners, hospital patients and other hangers-on associated with every out-station Boma. But Mpika was probably the only place in the world where taxes could be paid in caterpillars. What advantages we miss by being civilised! I wonder what his reaction would be if, in reply to my Final Demand, I presented my own Inspector of Taxes with a wheelbarrow-load of caterpillars.

Before leaving Mpika I went along to the cemetery to pay my respects to the memory of Charlie Ross, my predecessor, who was buried there. The cemetery was bleak and desolate. As I stood among the few quiet graves, four of whose occupants had met their death in the hunting field and whose bones had been brought back to the Boma to be buried, I reflected upon a legend I had heard some time before.

The Africans in this area have a belief that when a hunter is killed by an elephant the herd will come back at night and dance round the victim. It is a legend which seldom finds support in fact. But the night after Charlie Ross's body had been brought up from the Valley, four days' march away, a herd of elephants did, in fact, visit the Boma and were heard to trumpet near the cemetery. Elephants are very rarely seen within twenty miles of Mpika Boma but this uncanny experience was accepted as a matter of course by the people. Charlie Ross, who for years had tracked down marauding elephants in their villages, was a famous figure in the vicinity and it was only natural that the elephants should pay their last tribute to a daring hunter and a brave man.

8. A forgotten breed

High up on a windswept plateau two rivers rise within a stone's throw of each other; one flows eastward to the Luangwa, and eventually joins the Zambezi to make its way to the Indian Ocean; the other flows westward to the Luapula and the Congo to end its journey in the Atlantic. This is surely the very backbone of Africa.

My journey from Mpika to Kasama followed this continental divide through beautiful open moorland with deep running streams and occasional patches of forest at the headwaters of numerous springs. These dense forest patches are called 'mashitus' and are the last remnant of the rain-forest which completely covered this part of Central Africa thousands of years ago. It is interesting that certain wild creatures which inhabit these 'mashitus' are closely related to their rain-forest relatives in the Congo and the west coast of Africa many thousands of miles away and bear no resemblance to the typical local fauna. When the climate of this part of the world began to get drier, following the last glacial period, the rain-forests shrank, giving way to the open savannah and light woodland of today. There still remain, however, a few remnants of these forests on the high central plateau of Zambia which contain ancestors of the original fauna and flora of the past era. Isolation for thousands of years in these little islands of the old world has allowed mutations to alter the character of some of the small rodents, insects

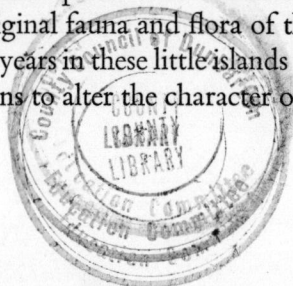

69

or birds, but they vary only slightly from their predecessors who still exist in the true rain-forests of West Africa. After all, a thousand years or so is a very short period in the evolution of a species.

One hundred and thirty miles and nine days later, I arrived in Kasama, which was the administrative headquarters of the Northern Province. It was a few days before Christmas when I reported to the Provincial Commissioner for duty and learned I was to make my headquarters at Luwingu, an out-station about a hundred miles westward on the northern shore of Lake Bangweulu, not because it was the most central place to operate from but because there happened to be a vacant house I could occupy there. This I thought to be an unnecessary luxury since most of my time was to be spent touring, but I did not question the decision. It was only later that I learnt the reason why the house was unoccupied.

The Province I was responsible for was as large as England. To help me deal with it I had a staff of twelve African Game Guards and one half-caste Game Scout as an assistant.

The Provincial Commissioner was most concerned when I said I wanted to start trekking to Luwingu the following day. He offered to put a truck at my disposal, to take me and my kit by road if I cared to stay over a few days, but I pleaded that I would prefer to see the country en route. He did not understand how anyone could prefer tramping through the bush in the rainy season to celebrating Christmas festivities in civilised surroundings. He thought I was nuts.

When I arrived at Luwingu I found the only white people on the station were the District Commissioner, Arthur Benson (later to be knighted and become Governor of the territory), and his family. They were very kind to me for the few days I remained at my headquarters and took endless trouble over me, although they were lacking an assistant. It was, in fact, the house of this assistant that I now occupied. He was, they told me candidly, a young cadet who had recently arrived from England with the bloom of youth still on his cheeks. They were less candid about the reason for his absence.

The assistant's name, I discovered, was Creighton-Burroughs. He had come to Luwingu only a couple of months before my own arrival, a conscientious young man who took the responsibilities of his position in the Native Administration very seriously. It was his duty he felt, to shoulder the white man's burden and to inspire the unenlightened inhabitants. He had made a study of the native language on his journey out and could make himself understood, albeit haltingly, after only a week in Africa.

To provide him with a companion and some light relief, the D.C.'s wife had given him a puppy from a rather mixed litter resulting from a misalliance between her pedigree spaniel and a local mongrel. To this he was devoted.

Things were going smoothly and it looked as if young Burroughs already had his feet planted on the bottom rung of the administrative ladder. But he reckoned without Ndevu. Ndevu was the 'mlonda', or night-watchman, a gnarled African ex-hunter. Not many days after his first safari, the D.C. invited Creighton-Burroughs to sundowners and pot-luck. Inevitably the only subject discussed was 'shop' and, after a polite interval, when coffee was cleared, Burroughs collected his hurricane lamp from the veranda, turned up the wick which was burning low, and walked across the station grounds to his house about a quarter of a mile away. He probably intended to work. In fact, he went to sleep.

He was awakened in the middle of the night by the most unholy uproar. Chairs and tables were being flung about as though a tornado had broken loose in the house. The puppy was emitting terror-stricken yowls and some large animal appeared to be running amuck in the debris. From the sitting-room, down the passage and towards his bedroom, the tornado gathered momentum. Burroughs only had time to reach under his mosquito-net for his torch on the bedside table when the bedroom door burst open and in rushed the puppy pursued by a huge lumbering shape.

Bedlam reigned. Down crashed the dressing-table. The beam of Burroughs's torch wavered for a second on the tawny form of a lion which had just taken a swipe at the puppy now cowering behind the upturned dressing-table. Burroughs, stunned, could only let out a watery scream.

It was this that Ndevu, who was employed for such emergencies, heard above the commotion. He left his nightly rounds and doubled over to give a hand.

By this time the Bwana was nearly coherent and yelled to the *mlonda* in several languages that there was a lion in the room. Undaunted, Ndevu pushed his shot-gun through the mosquito gauze on the window and blindly pulled the trigger.

There was a deafening explosion. The lion, terrified, bolted through the door and out through the veranda, never to be seen again. The puppy remained motionless behind the dressing-table.

Inside, there was an ominous silence. Cautiously Ndevu crept in. He was beginning to have second thoughts about the wisdom of firing, at point-blank range, into a darkened room.

His doubts were soon confirmed. For there on the bed, doubled up and quite beyond speech in any language, lay Burroughs. He was admitted to hospital with severe wounds in the softest part of his body, and it was weeks before all the pellets were removed and he was able once again to take the weight off his feet during meals. To my infinite regret I never met him. By the time he returned I had gone.

For after a week in Luwinga Boma I found myself on the march again with a team of twenty-five carriers and supplies to last up to three or four months. As the whole province was new to me I wanted to cover as much territory as possible in one long foot tour, taking in the most important game areas on the way.

The first stage took us southward along the north and north-west shores of Lake Bangweulu, then westwards to Fort Roseberry, a small settlement 120 miles from our starting-point. We then continued northwards to Kawambwa, another district Boma, which we reached after eight days' walk.

Kawambwa was a pleasant little out-station, consisting of half-a-dozen families and situated on a high moorland in delightful surroundings overlooking rolling grasslands punctuated with an occasional 'mashitu'. All these out-stations provided an equipped rest-house, which I was glad to occupy for a few days as a change from my tent camp. According to custom, I called on the District Commissioner to learn what I could about his district, especially about the distribution of game animals. He told me a group of elephants were raiding the cassava gardens among the villages on the shores of Lake Mweru. An African hunter had been posted to the area but had had no success in shooting any of the elephants.

Before setting off to try and improve on his luck I spent a pleasant visit there, relaxing in the evening over the inevitable sundowners and enjoying the hospitality of these generous people who, like most of those who live in small communities, could not go to enough trouble to make a newcomer feel welcome and at ease.

From Kawambwa I travelled a short distance to the Luapula

and followed it to where it feeds Lake Mweru. The Luapula is a deep, slow-flowing river, somewhat wider than the Thames below Tower Bridge. After draining the waters of Bangweulu it flows due south, then forms a hairpin bend and flows northwards to feed Lake Mweru; flowing out from the north end of the lake into the Belgian Congo it changes its name to Lualaba and eventually becomes the Congo River.

I found the wildlife in the Northern Province very disappointing compared to the Luangwa Valley. My interest in those days was centred around the larger animals, particularly the dangerous ones, so I looked forward to some action on reaching the villages on the lake shore where elephant raiding was reported.

When I arrived there, however, I realised why the hunter had had no success: the 'mateshi' bush – a very dense thicket – grew right down to the water's edge and the gardens were literally hacked out of the bush, which made a solid wall enclosing the cultivated patches. The elephants lived in this very extensive thicket and only came out at night when they felt like a change of diet. They enjoyed complete immunity from reprisals as it was more than the average hunter would do to follow them into their retreat where visibility was only a few yards. This was the densest thicket I have ever known; the interlacing vines were practically impenetrable, yet the elephant could use its strength to force a passage through and the resilient branches would spring back into place, closing the tunnel to any lesser animal.

I camped among these villages for nearly a week and shot three elephants, much to the delight of the local inhabitants and of my own carriers who had been without meat for some time, but not to my own enjoyment. Two days later I reached the international border between Northern Rhodesia and the

Belgian Congo, or rather the compromise boundary agreed upon by the two D.C.s concerned: in point of fact the border at that time was in dispute. I had now walked in easy stages, with several interruptions, from Fort Jameson near the Nyasaland–Portuguese border to the Congo border, albeit by a very indirect and devious route – a total distance of nearly one thousand miles.

It was in this area, between Lake Mweru and Mweru Marsh, after I had been on tour for nearly three months, that I first met Carruthers. Like Burroughs, he was a cadet and had recently arrived in the country. This was his first 'ulendo' (a word synonymous with *safari*: the latter word is, as a matter of fact, a very recent introduction from East Africa). He had walked up from Mporokoso Boma seven days' journey off, and had been told to look out for me to tell me that I was to report to Zomba, the capital of Nyasaland, for military service.

Perhaps a latent streak of jealousy tinged my attitude towards young Carruthers. Reluctantly I had to concede that he possessed most of the qualities that make up the best type of Englishman. But his hair was just that little bit too long and his clothes were a little too perfectly casual. I had the impression that a good deal of thought and planning must have gone into his choice of wardrobe. His accent and phraseology were, of course, impeccable.

When he joined the Provincial Administration from Cambridge, Carruthers felt proud to have been selected to play a part in building an empire. He became convinced that it was an honour as well as a duty to pass on his superior attainments to those who had not had his advantages. No one could accuse him of being deliberately condescending but to my prejudiced mind he appeared that bit too precious. I was forced, however, to admire his enthusiasm. He was certainly very enthusiastic about his first 'ulendo': Sanders of the River and all that!

He duly invited me to his camp and I enjoyed a superb four-course dinner; this I appreciated all the more because my supplies were running short and I was getting rather tired of living off the land. It was towards the end of dinner that he told me how on the previous day he had become lost and was forced to spend a very uncomfortable night up a tree. When he told me the story I had to admit that he treated the whole incident with admirable fortitude and a commendable sense of humour, but it was only later, when chatting with some of my boys on the shores of Lake Mweru, that I was able to fill in all the details. I could imagine his consternation.

Apparently, during the afternoon before I met him young Carruthers had decided to go for a stroll around camp and then shoot a brace of guinea-fowl for the pot. He felt confident he could find his way without a guide if he kept close to camp. So, taking his double-barrel Purdey he strode off, thrilled at the thought of his first outing alone in Africa. He would make a circuit around camp, skirting the large 'dambo'* and come in from the south.

When the sun was getting low he thought he must be within sight of camp. He felt he had encircled the 'dambo' and should by now be in sight of his camp. This must be the same 'dambo' – but where was the tent? He couldn't possibly have lost his way – could he? Perhaps this was not the same one after all, for there should be a couple of rather conspicuous termite mounds which he would have easily recognised. There seemed to be a break in the trees on the other side, which indicated an open

* There is no proper English equivalent for this word. It can be described as an open meadow which serves as a drainage line at the head of a water-course and is usually waterlogged in the wet season.

space and was possibly what he was looking for. It was now getting dark but he refused to panic.

'Keep calm,' he told himself, 'sit down and think.' He remembered this advice from a book by one of the early African explorers. It was imperative he should not panic. With a mental effort he tried to re-trace his footsteps.

'I started off with the sun at my back,' he recalled, 'and slightly to my left; that means I was walking east by north-east for just about half an hour; I crossed the 'dambo', bearing right along its opposite fringe through some scattered terminalia scrub, and therefore reckoned I must have made a semi-circle of about three miles round camp. The glow from the setting sun was now on my left. The camp *must* be somewhere around here. Admittedly I lost direction when I went after those guinea-fowl about an hour after starting. Perhaps if I continued in this direction I would see a fire or hear the boys chattering. I could never, of course, let off a shot or call for help: that would be an admission of gross incompetence and a very poor show. One has to keep up an appearance and set a good example in front of these chaps. After all, I mustn't admit that the new District Officer is incapable of going out without a nurse.'

As it got darker he began to remember some of the tales he had been told about man-eaters. Only that morning his District Messenger had shown him the pug-marks of a lion near the stream they crossed before pitching camp. It was now quite dark and he could only see the outlines of the bushes against the starlit sky: a frightening number of them assumed the shape of elephants and crouching predators ready to pounce. A hyena howled plaintively in the distance. Although it was some way off it was quite probable that its mate would be hunting parallel on this very route. He began to move a trifle faster.

A sudden crashing of a large animal through the bushes in

front decided Carruthers. He was a fairly tough youngster, and he knew he was letting his side down, but he had to admit to himself at last that he was extremely frightened. The only sensible thing to do was to climb a tree and wait for daylight.

It was as cold as it can be in June, the chill from the 'dambo' rising up to penetrate his very bone marrow. It was uncomfortable, too, in the fork of the fig tree and the mosquitoes were driving him crazy. The night seemed endless.

Eventually, and very gradually, the eastern sky became imperceptibly lighter and slowly the world became visible. His whole body ached from squatting in so unnatural a position; as he was stretching his legs to get his blood circulating before descending from his perch he saw below him, to his utter astonishment, his own houseboy immaculately dressed in his white uniform and carrying a tray, appear out of a clump of bushes.

'Good morning, Bwana,' he said. 'I have brought your early-morning tea.'

For the bush out of which he had appeared concealed his own kitchen tent, but who was a mere servant to question the ways of a white man?

My next meeting with Carruthers took place many years later when he was a Provincial Commissioner. Soon after I met him, he too received his call-up papers and joined the R.A.F. where he blazed a distinguished war career as a Battle of Britain pilot, earning the D.F.C. and bar. I was glad that by then I had grown wholeheartedly to like him. He belongs, like Burroughs, to a forgotten breed: the stuff of Empire-builders.

9. Marauders

Once I joined the Army I thought my hunting days were over, at least for the duration of the war. But this did not turn out to be the case. Lions, it so happened, had been killing cattle at Chief Mlumbe's village ten miles north of Zomba, shortly after my arrival there. It was the second kill in three days.

Directly I heard of this I obtained permission from my Commanding Officer to go to the scene and investigate. I found the remains of an ox which had been dragged from the cattle kraal, and I felt fairly confident that the lion would return to finish his meal that night. The signs were undoubtedly those of a large male lion which had squeezed through a gap in the pole stockade, killed a young ox and dragged it over the eight-foot fence. It had partially consumed the victim in the open gardens beyond.

I left a guard over the remains and returned again at sundown to take up my position for the night. For the occasion I had borrowed an ancient two-seater car from which I had removed the windscreen and hood in order to give me an all-round field of fire. I placed this about twenty yards downwind of the carcass and directed the headlamps at the remains. I had made up my mind to wait until the lion really settled down to its feed before switching on the headlamps.

It was a brilliant moonlit night of the sort that occurs only in the tropics, and I was comfortably settled in the front seat with my rifle across the bonnet ready for immediate action. At first I was alert, full of anticipation. But after a while my attention slipped, my mind adrift on a placid lake of contentment. On such a night one's thoughts seem suspended and memories lap against one's consciousness, not imperiously but invitingly, like waves on a tranquil shore. A deep sense of peace prevailed and subdued murmurs from the nearby huts, like the faint sound of the surf on a lake shore, lulled my senses. I was not part of the scene.

A movement in the shadows near a small acacia tree abruptly reminded me where I was. I rallied my wits, stealthily reached for my rifle and slid the safety-catch forward. The shadow had taken shape but it was too far away for me to recognise. It was coming diagonally towards me and would soon appear in the open moonlit space. I reminded myself again not to shoot until the lion had settled down and was well advanced with its meal, when it would become less cautious and allow me a steadier shot.

Then I saw the second shadowy form. This could not be the lion I was waiting for, there had only been one killer when I checked the spoor in the morning. These must be a couple of scavenging hyenas who had picked up the scent and were about to feast on the lion's kill. I had to adjust my plan quickly. The hyenas would almost certainly drag the carcass off into the bushes – out of range for when the lion eventually came. I could not, of course, let off a shot to drive them away. I did not even wish to shine my torch for fear of disturbing the lion should he be in the vicinity. And I felt sure he was. Hyenas are cowardly creatures and never attack an active person, so I quickly leaped over the side of the car and picked up a couple of clods of earth to drive them away. I waited until the first figure was about to come into the open and then rushed at it, making the appropriate shooing noises and hurling the missile at it. My attack was so unexpected that the bewildered animal went off like a scalded cat. (The phrase 'with his tail between his legs' comes to mind but honesty compels me to admit that I could not see his tail in the moonlight!) His companion did not bother to find out what it was all about and rushed off as I launched a second clod of earth to help him on his way.

I felt very pleased to have settled their hash but knowing the habits of hyenas I fully expected them to skulk around and make another attempt later. Hyenas have no pride and never know when they are unwelcome.

I returned to my post, but somehow things did not seem so peaceful any more. A few clouds were banking up in the east. I waited one hour. Then another. It looked as if the lion had decided not to return that night. The moon clouded over and a drizzle began. I even started to hope that the hyenas would return, just to relieve the monotony. It was no longer any fun, but I felt I had to stick it out now until dawn.

The light rain cleared up a little about 3 a.m. but the sky remained overcast. I moved restlessly, sensing the dawn.

Just before dawn there is an ominous, foreboding feeling in the air – when night is finished but day has not yet taken over. There is no visible change in the sky but the feeling is un-mistakably there. The animals and insects sense it. The night-jars cease their chirrup-chirrup and the ground hornbills take over with their peculiar drum-like call, drumming out the rendezvous from which to start their dawn patrols. Even the cockerels who have been locked up in a dark hut all night will herald their awareness that a new day is about to be born.

It was during this vacuum that I heard a barely perceptible rustle in the bushes. Was I imagining it? No; the sound was closer this time and more distinct as the animal came towards the bait. A long silence. Then I could hear a slobbering eating noise; then a distinct crunching of bone. There is quite a difference between the feeding noises of a hyena and a lion at twenty yards, and I knew my wait had not been in vain. Give him another two minutes, I told myself. But two minutes in such circumstances seem an eternity. I groped for the light switch and in the blaze that followed he was facing me like a naughty boy surprised at the larder. My rifle was lined up and when I fired he crumpled where he stood.

As my shot rang out a dark shadow seemed to move on the other side of the carcass. But when I looked more closely it had gone, merging into the other shadows around it. I had probably imagined it.

I turned in response to the uproar from the adjacent village: joyous pandemonium at the thought of the cattle-slayer at last meeting its just fate. Soon after, the first pale light of dawn brought the surroundings into focus and one or two of the bolder villagers left their huts and came to learn what had happened. Rather than skin the lion, I had it loaded on to the old car and was about to drive back to Zomba with it when I remembered the hyenas and decided to check over their spoor. There were their tracks, disappearing side by side into the bush. I went over to inspect them. Imagine my utter astonishment when instead of the dog-like impressions I expected I saw the unmistakable pug marks of two lions. The shadow I had seen had not been my imagination.

For a long time afterwards I wondered why a lion, who can slay a buffalo, should scurry away like a scared cat when suddenly confronted by a human who aims a clod of earth at it, especially at night when the lion dominates the darkness. I have since had more experience of lions and realise how cautious they can be when deliberately approaching their prey. They will go to endless trouble to manœuvre into strategic positions and can be tremendously bold in their planned attacks, but they will invariably retreat from any sudden, unexpected action.

10. Namwera man-eaters

The episode I have just described was not the only lion hunt I was involved in during my military career. The second was more serious – and it had tragic consequences.

Some months later I found myself stationed at a military camp on the Nyasaland–Portuguese border near Lake Nyasa. Namwera was a fairly well populated native area in the district of Fort Johnston, consisting mostly of typical savannah woodland. The grass which covered the uncultivated land was rank and tall, reaching above a man's head. Later in the year, when the dry season advanced, annual bush fires would sweep through the country burning all the cover and improving visibility; but for the present the grass offered ideal cover for lions and other predators.

A few elephants roamed the hills between our camp and the lake but most of the game, except for bush-pigs and baboons, had been shot out by local hunters. Occasionally lions visited the area from across the border and, finding it difficult to secure their normal prey, would sometimes turn to the only other available food: man. Once they learnt how tasty human flesh was and how easy to procure, they became habitual man-eaters. This is the normal pattern that leads up to man-killing, although some lions suffering from physical defects do kill humans because they are unable to tackle any more agile prey.

These outbreaks of man-eating used to occur from time to

time in this part of Nyasaland, spreading terror among the local inhabitants. It is not only the fear of death which terrifies them, for most primitive people are notoriously fatalistic, it is the fear of the supernatural, which permeates their moral fibre and undermines all their natural courage.

The lives of primitive natives are dominated by witchcraft and any misfortune which befalls the community is said to have been caused by spirits who have returned to seek vengeance for some misdeed. There is no such thing as a *natural* death: every person who dies is considered the victim of some evil influence and this influence can extend to the whole community. No expiation is possible except by the appropriate sacrifices.

On this particular occasion the villagers naturally ascribed the outbreak of man-eating to some vengeful spirit, though it was rather worse than anything they had previously experienced. All the witch-doctor's exhortations were in vain. It was obvious that the spirit of the Chief's ancestor was very angry and had returned in the shape of a lion to punish them. Such a spirit-lion is called 'Walenga'.

At this time I was in charge of an infantry company of African troops who had just completed their recruits' training and were waiting to be drafted to the front-line units in the Abyssinian war-zone. One morning after I had sent my men off on field exercises I returned to my office to clear up some 'admin.' work which was long overdue, and had just settled down to the hated task of preparing returns, when a colleague of mine, Dusty Miller, put his head round the door and said: 'The C.O. wants to see you rather urgently.'

Dusty had a very handsome moustache of which he was inordinately proud and three pips on his shoulder of which he was even more proud. He was Officer-in-Charge of 'B' Company and had the office next to mine (if a pole and mud construction with a thatch roof could be called by such a name).

'Blast! I suppose old Bingo is getting ants because I haven't submitted these damned training schedules. How the hell does he expect me to train my men and do the administrative work when he takes my Clerk away? No one ever reads the bloody things anyway.'

Dusty's moustache bristled rather disapprovingly. He was new to the Detachment and did not quite approve of the familiar manner in which we colonials spoke of our Commanding Officer. Dusty had been a regular soldier in the Brigade of Guards, had risen from the ranks and was consequently a stickler for etiquette. To him the Commanding Officer was on speaking terms with God.

'As a matter of fact,' Dusty said knowingly, 'it isn't about your returns. He's worried about those man-eaters. Another message has come in from Chief Kawinga and the runners are in his office now.'

'What the hell does he expect me to do about it?' I replied. 'Perhaps he hasn't heard there's a war on.'

I liked to rankle Dusty Miller when he adopted this rather supercilious attitude.

'I don't know, but don't you think you had better go along and find out?'

I knocked on the door marked 'Commanding Officer', saluted formally and stood to attention in front of Colonel Murray's desk until I was ordered to stand at ease.

'Morning, Carr.'

'Good morning, sir.'

This was Colonel Murray's second war. He walked with a limp which was caused by an H.E. shell which had exploded beside him on the Ypres front twenty-five years previously. He tried hard to justify his quite underserved reputation for irascibility and sometimes succeeded in cowing some of the junior subalterns, but those of us who knew him better realised that his temper was a fraud which masked a benevolent feeling towards his unit and staff.

'You're supposed to be a big-game hunter, aren't you?' he barked at me.

'Who said so, sir?'

'Well, dammit, you were a Game Ranger or something, weren't you, before you joined up?'

'Yes, sir, I was.'

'Well then, dammit man, you must know something about hunting.'

'Yes, sir.'

'Then why the devil didn't you say so in the first place instead of wasting my time?'

Having done justice to his reputation as a fire-eater, the C.O. felt he could relax. I knew his technique pretty well by now.

'I have just had another message from Chief Kawinga. You've heard all about these man-eating lions? They've now killed two more women in Msuku's village and the Chief asks us to do something about it. That makes another five deaths this week. Would you go out after them? You can hand your Company over to your Second-in-Command for a couple of days.'

Of course I jumped at the chance to get into the bush again.

'All right, Carr, I'll leave it to you. You'd better interrogate the two villagers who brought in the report. Any further messages that come in I'll leave for you to handle.'

I took the emissaries to my office and, while they squatted on the earth floor, listened to their story. They were typically dressed with a length of cloth wrapped round their lower limbs

87

and twisted into a roll around their middles, exposing their navels. Their glistening bodies had not dried off from the exertion of their five-mile jog-trot from the Chief's village. The older of the two, who acted as spokesman, was a dignified, white-haired old man whose skin was parched and crinkled like a dried apple through sixty-odd years of exposure to the African sun. Both carried spears, which they had left outside in accordance with traditional courtesy – stuck, blade upwards, in the ground. The two of them contrasted noticeably with the young recruits who were marching about the parade-ground in khaki shorts, spotless white shirts and pill-box hats.

I already knew the story of the earlier casualties but purposely allowed my messengers to reconstruct each episode in their own way. The man-eaters had been at large for some time in the district but we at the camp had not taken particular notice until a night-watchman employed by one of the European tobacco-farmers only two miles away had been killed whilst tending the fires in the tobacco barns. Only his head remained to tell the gruesome tale next morning.

A few days later two natives were killed riding a bicycle near by. And now this third report brought us up-to-date with news of the latest killing in Msuku's village.

The lions had killed a woman and child, dragging the woman's body from her hut into the long grass nearby, where they had eaten her. The second child in the hut had escaped unhurt. The screams aroused the occupants of the other huts in the village, but in the darkness and confusion they could do little about it. Someone had set alight one of the thatched huts to illuminate the scene. No doubt the combination of the blaze, the shouting and the drum-beating helped to boost the villagers' morale and gave them a sense of security from further attack. But they could do nothing to drive off the lions, who could be

'The melancholy cry of the Fish Eagle remains in my memory as typical of the Luangwa.' Below, a serval cat rarely seen during the day

'You might catch sight of some of the night prowlers returning to their hide-out'

'In all my experience I have never heard of another such bold, frenzied, attack upon a hut'

heard in the tall grass crunching the bones of their victims. The whole population spent the rest of the night in terror, barricaded inside two of the stoutest huts.

After hearing this story I decided to go out immediately before the spoor was stale. I borrowed a light truck from the Battalion Transport Officer and was soon on my way to Msuku's village, accompanied by the two messengers. The village was in a pathetic state, the women mournfully wailing round the headman's hut and the men hanging around helplessly. The charred remains of a hut were still smouldering like a funeral pyre and cast a miserable ghostly blue haze over the whole scene.

The nightmare of events could be reconstructed from the spoor. Two lions had entered the village from the east and had carefully circled the hut before one of them had broken through the rather flimsy pole-and-grass structure. The signs showed where the body had been dragged from the hut into the surrounding grass, and we could see the trail of flattened grass left in their wake. None of the villagers had dared follow the lions, who now felt perfectly secure in their hiding-place. It was up to someone to disillusion them.

I had brought with me one of my African N.C.O.s, Sergeant Liasala, as a tracker and gun-bearer and the two of us followed the spoor, which at first was a clearly defined drag mark. Emboldened now by the presence of two rifles, a few of the more stalwart villagers collected their spears and tried to follow behind us. I remonstrated with them and sent them back, since we had to move as stealthily as possible. Along the trail, with the sound of voices still audible from the village, we came across the place where the lions had first settled down to eat. The body of the woman had been disembowelled and the stomach contents put out of the way and covered with grass, which is a typical habit of feeding lions. The victim's clothing was scattered around but there was no sign of the rest of her body, which the lions must have picked up and carried further on.

There were no further drag marks, so the trail through the eight-foot grass was now less obvious. In addition visibility was reduced to only a few yards. We had to go in single file. Liasala stayed close behind me, armed with a spare rifle. We inched our way forward one step at a time: a long pause to listen, then another step. There was no wind to carry our scent for no air seemed to circulate at all among these towering grass stems; all was motionless.

We had not gone more than a hundred yards when we suddenly heard a grunt as the lions crashed through the grass a few yards ahead. I sank on my knees and pointed my rifle in the direction of the noise, not knowing which way they were breaking. They had heard us when we were nearly on top of them and bounded off. Seconds later we came on their resting-place and the remains of their feast. Only part of an arm, the leg bones, and the head remained.

We continued stepping carefully, knowing we would not get a glimpse of the lions unless the grass thinned out ahead. Again another grunt, very close this time, as they bounded off once more. They had full bellies and now presumably wanted to find somewhere quiet to digest their meal in peace. Once more we flushed them and then miraculously the trail took us into more open woodland. Knowing they were being hunted they kept on the move into valley and over hill, giving us neither glimpse nor sound of them, even though we were close on their track. By late afternoon I decided to give up and return to our truck before dark. It had been a most disappointing and tiring day, but I was all the more determined to continue the

hunt next morning. We arrived back at camp long after
sunset.

Early next morning two natives arrived to report another
killing at Kapito's village. This time it was a native man who
had strayed to the outskirts of the village; he had been pounced
upon, dragged off and devoured.

I had half-expected, half-dreaded such news. I collected
Liasala and we were soon on the way to Kapito's village, which
was not far from where we had left off the hunt the previous
afternoon. We followed practically the same procedure as the
previous day and soon flushed the lions in the long grass where
they had been lying up.

It was then that I looked upon the most horrible sight I have
ever seen: the body of the victim had been completely devoured
except for the skull, from which all the flesh had been torn
leaving a clean white mask, and from the eye-socket stared one
stark, lidless eye.

Twice more we flushed these lions and then I realised how
hopeless it was to try to play hide-and-seek with such creatures
when all they had to do was listen for our approach and
keep one stage ahead all the time. Everything was in their
favour. There was only one alternative: to drive them with
beaters.

I decided to improvise a drive with all the able-bodied men
I could muster. I took up a stand in the clearest ground I could
find and sent all the faint-hearted villagers round in a semi-
circle to drive the lions on to me. This turned out to be a flop.
Naturally enough, I suppose, the beaters were reluctant to fan
out and in any case I could not cover the whole front in such
close country. As a result the lions broke through on one flank
and I did not see or hear them.

I decided to call the hunt off and return next day with my

whole company of askari, two hundred strong, and let them be my beaters. The C.O. had no objection to the plan and I had them all standing-to next morning, waiting for the anticipated tidings. None came. The following day, however, a messenger came on a bicycle and told us how the lions had tried to break into a hut at Mtola's village but had been driven off. That is what we were waiting for. My men were excited and anxious to prove themselves; this was far more fun than slogging around doing field exercises.

I marched at a brisk pace at the head of my company and we soon covered the five miles to Mtola's village. All the men were armed with rifles and bayonets but I had not issued ammunition. Some distance before the village I let them fall out and sit quietly whilst Sergeant Liasala and I went forward to investigate.

At Mtola's village we were told of the terrifying ordeal the inhabitants had been through that night. I could verify from the tracks that only one lion had been on the prowl that night, so I presumed the pair had split up and gone hunting separately.

All had taken place in ominous silence. In fact these lions never once used their hunting grunts (it would be wrong to call them roars) during all these days, as they would normally have done if hunting in a well-stocked game area. I have often noticed that habitual man-eaters, or stock killers, are mute when prowling.

The single lion had arrived near the village before sundown and the beaten-down nest in the grass showed where he had bided his time till dark. From dusk on a reign of terror ruled in Mtola's village. Since these outbreaks started the villagers had wisely resorted to communal protection at nights. Instead of each family sleeping in their own huts with the unmarried girls and boys in separate huts, as is customary, they now selected the strongest huts in the village and packed in together, barricading the doors against their foe.

Soon after sunset the lion began to prowl. He tried to force an entry into one of the huts but was disappointed to find it empty after knocking down the door. He then carried out a general inspection from hut to hut. As he sniffed for an opening, a subdued, hardly perceptible, grunting kept the cooped-up occupants informed of his route. A bold onslaught was made upon one hut but the shouting from the dozen occupants within was too much for him and he moved on. Undaunted, however, his tracks showed his determination not to leave without a meal. Another hut was broken into but again it was fortunately empty except for half-a-dozen fowls, two of which the lion killed and proceeded to eat. This satisfied him for an hour or so and the signs showed where he had rested outside in a blooded, befeathered bed. However, this was only an aperitif and he made one last desperate attack on Mtola's own hut, which was harbouring the headman, his family and half-a-dozen others.

In spite of the constant shouting inside he would not be driven off and hammered to such purpose that he smashed the wooden cross-beam which held the door in position. It was only the combined weight of the occupants pushing against the weight of the lion from inside which kept the door in place. When Mtola saw that the door could not withstand the onslaught any longer he shouted to his men in an adjacent hut. They rallied together and after setting fire to an empty hut to provide adequate light began waving flaming brands from the fire. Then they drove the lion from the doorway with their spears.

In all my experience of lions, particularly of man-eaters, I have never heard of another such bold, frenzied attack upon an occupied house. I have known lions on rare occasions make attempts to break into huts but even then they usually try to sneak in stealthily through a gap. Most man-eaters will lie in wait and take a woman going to water or an unsuspecting person sleeping by the fireside, but very rarely indeed do they 'huff and puff and blow the house down' as did the wolf in the classic fable.

We had no difficulty in following the lion's spoor from Mtola's village, since it kept to the path. The tracks led us to a small, low-lying 'dambo' with short, luscious, green grass, which was in pleasing contrast to the monotonous brown-yellow grass we had been travelling through. The path across the 'dambo' was damp and the lion spoor showed up boldly like jelly moulds in the soft mud. At the water-hole we met two women drawing water whilst their menfolk protected them with poised spears. We were told that a lion had passed through their (Mpata's) village just before dawn. It was probably the mate of the one we were spooring, for a little farther on the two joined forces and continued on into the protective cover of the towering grass.

Once we had located them I returned to the village to make my plan. I had guessed that the lions would lay low for the rest of the day and I was in no hurry. With Sergeant Liasala I took the village headman and one of his elders and made a thorough survey of the locality. There was a criss-cross of paths in all directions and we had no trouble encircling the area where we had left the lions.

One flank of the area bordered fairly open woodland and offered good visibility, so I decided to make this my base-line. Once we had completely encircled the area with beaters we would drive towards the base-line where I would place my riflemen.

I then returned to my askari and selected a dozen of my best marksmen, to each of whom I issued five rounds of ammunition. They were placed in convenient trees along the base-line, roughly twenty yards apart.

We then returned for the remainder of the askari, who were waiting in the village, and rounded up more volunteers from the adjoining villages. These were to be our beaters. We divided them into several parties, each under the command of an African N.C.O. Calling up each party in turn, we placed the beaters with fixed bayonets and spears in a circle facing inwards so that the lions were completely cordoned off. At a signal the beaters were to advance evenly, keeping station on their N.C.O.s, towards the base-line, shouting and making as much noise as they wished with the idea of driving the lions on to the guns. In order to allow me time to get back into position with the riflemen I gave them five minutes before starting.

I was determined to be in at the kill and also to be on hand should either of the lions be wounded and have to be dispatched. My recruits, though well trained in the use of rifles, were inexperienced. It is one thing to be able to put up a good score on the rifle range but quite a different matter to fire at a running lion from a cramped position in a tree. I now took up a safe position in a tree about midway along the base-line to avoid any stray bullets.

I was still out of breath from my scamper back but saw that there were still a couple of minutes to go before the drive commenced. On the dot the signal shot was fired and the noise from the beaters half a mile away was shattering. The lions must have been very surprised to hear this simultaneous uproar coming from all around them. But not exactly all around them: there was a gap ahead and it was here that I hoped they would choose to escape.

I began to feel anxious. Surely with all that hullabaloo to

hasten them along they should have broken through by now. I was deaf to all the noise; there was only one sound I wanted to hear and that was a rifle-shot from one of the men in the trees. Had I slipped up when placing the beaters and missed the spoor which took the lions outside our cordon? No, I had been particularly careful about this, and Liasala, who was a good tracker, had also thoroughly rechecked. I was becoming despondent and imagined all my preparation to be wasted. The beaters seemed too close already and in a few seconds would reach our base-line.

Then suddenly a shot! And another! And again! My mood changed to exultation. We'd won! The shots came from the extreme right flank of my base-line near the gardens so I ran there as fast as I could, hurdling boulders and breaking through thorns and small bushes. The armed askari in the trees had instructions to keep to their posts till called.

There was a crowd of beaters gesticulating wildly around the post where the lions had broken through but I could see no tawny corpses. The lions had passed through a few yards in front of the beaters. As they came into the open, a youngster, Private Willard, took a shot from his perch at the first lion and bowled it over but it had struggled up and bounded away. As its mate followed, Willard aimed two hurried shots. He said they went home but I think his enthusiasm got the better of his truthfulness. The lions had come into the open calmly and deliberately, one after the other, not knowing the trap set for them and intending to outflank the bothersome noise. Had the noise been less persistent they might have decided to try and face it, but more than two hundred howling human beings must have been discouraging even to these outrageously bold animals.

After they had been shot at, the lions had bounded across the open and into the cover beyond. The blood spoor from the wounded lion was clearly visible and the marks on the ground showed where he had been knocked over and pawed the ground in his rage. The two shots at the other lion, in spite of our hero's assurances, were, I surmised, a bit wild.

I made a reconnaissance in a wide circle and determined that both the lions were hiding in the thicket ahead and that at least one of them would be very angry. Two courses were open: the obvious one was to follow the lions into the cover, but this was needlessly risky; the alternative was to drive them into the open once more. I decided on the safer method. I quickly improvised another drive, using the same encircling tactics but on a far smaller scale. We had no time for a thorough reconnaissance. While I was placing the beaters we saw the heavy blood spoor of the wounded lion. He had left his cover and broken the encircling trap, so this drive had to be called off.

Leaving instructions for the company to stand by, Liasala and I again took up the spoor. The blood was thick and every few hundred yards the wounded lion would lie down, leaving a pool of blood. I judged the wound to be low on the left side, probably in the thigh. Liasala had shown his merit as a tracker but when we got into thick cover and had to go single file he hung back and tried to persuade me to give up. In the more open spaces he would do the tracking but when we came to very thick vegetation and had to travel single file, it was me who had to lead. The danger of spooring for yourself is that you must keep your eyes concentrating on the ground, and so you cannot give full attention to what lies ahead. This tense concentration can be very exhausting.

To relate the rest of the chase in detail would be tedious, although there was nothing tedious about it at the time. One of the greatest thrills of hunting is to be hot on the spoor with your nerves expectantly on edge. We kept up a close pursuit and on two occasions came near enough to hear the lions crashing on ahead. I could not understand why after last night's audacious display one of them did not decide to make a stand and settle with his pursuers. I had become so weary that I almost hoped he would decide on this course of action. I certainly had no desire to go through the whole performance again next day. I prayed that if he did make a stand he would choose a fairly open stretch of country.

The sun was getting low over the Kafindi hills, and I was beginning to lose all hope when the tracks suddenly swung away to the east towards the Portuguese border, leaving the grass country. The trail took us through the gardens of a small village nestling snugly in a pass less than half a mile from the international border. It was a picturesque village, hidden among fresh banana groves. We were now in the higher ground which was covered by scrub bush and small, spiky comiphera bushes. Here the terrain becomes stonier as it rises gently towards the foothills. But, glory be, no tall grass!

There was barely a quarter of an hour of light left before darkness fell, and then, quite unexpectedly, Liasala saw the lion limping badly and disappearing among a cluster of trees some way ahead. I rushed forward, but was only able to get in a crippling shot from behind which merely anchored him. As I approached, he crouched snarling with all the concentrated fury of a killer. As he tried to build up enough strength for that last desperate spring his tail lashed from side to side and his eyes blazed aggression. But he was exhausted and physically incapable of this final effort. I shot him where he crouched.

As for the second lion, it is sufficient to say we tracked him down on three successive days, using the same tactics with beaters and riflemen, until eventually he followed the same fate as his companion.

Namwera was rid of its terror and the people were embarrassingly grateful. These two lions had been responsible for eleven victims in two weeks. And it is not known how many others may have succumbed to them elsewhere. Both lions were in their prime, which disproves the theory that only those which are too old or unable to catch wild game will eat human flesh. In this case, obviously, they had started to kill man because man had killed off the wild game which is their natural diet.

Liasala and I became local heroes and Kawinga, the big chief of the district, offered to give me land for a farm if I would come and live in his country: a gesture which, I would like to think, has never been repeated to another white man.

CHANGE OF HEART

11. The honey-guide

This is not the place to describe my military career, which in any case was not so remarkable. I will leap-frog five years to the time of my discharge from the Army when I was again posted to Fort Jameson, the gateway to Luangwa Valley.

By this time a Game Department had been established which was responsible for many other aspects of wildlife conservation besides elephant control. Throughout the territory numerous wildlife areas had been proclaimed and the emphasis now lay more on the conservation and enforcement of the game laws than on the 'control' of destructive animals.

The system I had previously inaugurated for training African hunters ('fundis') to take over elephant control had been continued, so that the European Game Ranger no longer had to spend all his time tracking down marauding elephants; he could leave this to his subordinate staff and devote his time to more constructive measures.

Times were changing. The Jeep, which had been designed for warfare, found a new use in opening up country which previously could only be traversed on foot. My own outlook on the sort of life I was leading was also undergoing a change.

As the months and years went by I began to notice things I never knew existed. I began to take a more critical interest in the ecology of my environment. Trees, which at one time were just a lovely part of the scene, began to take shape and acquire botanical names. I began to see a relationship between the types of soil and the vegetation, and between the vegetation and the animals. I began to appreciate, although rather imperfectly, the relationship between the different species – how one depends upon the other and how each particular species fills a niche in the habitat. I was being initiated into the mysterious ways of nature.

As some of these secrets began to unfold, my interest in hunting became correspondingly less. To observe the habits of these creatures, to try to puzzle out what it all meant, now became exciting. It was no longer only the larger, dangerous animals that appealed to me.

One of the more intriguing of the smaller creatures I took an interest in was 'Nsulu' – the honey-guide. Its scientific name is, very appropriately, *Indicator indicator*. This bird actually leads man to honey. And in doing so it poses an interesting evolutionary problem. Did it learn the habit recently with the advent of man (a relative newcomer in terms of evolution), or has it adapted a much older innate habit which was previously used to guide other honey-eating animals to the hives?

The honey-guide is a small, rather drab, insignificant bird about the size of a common sparrow. Its plain browny-grey colour is relieved by a dirty yellow patch on each shoulder; its white outer tail-feathers are quite conspicuous when in flight, and these are said to be an additional aid to those it is guiding – a sort of tail light which makes life easier for honey-hunters. Nsulu is found all over Central Africa except in the equatorial forests and deserts. In the *brachystegia* woodland of Zambia, where honey is plentiful, it is particularly common and seems to know where to find every beehive in a very wide area. It will range the forests ceaselessly until it encounters man and then, after seducing him away from his legitimate business, will lead him unerringly to the nearest hive, which may be several miles away. The honey-guide has no means of procuring its favourite food without the help of man, because these hives are invariably found deep in the centre of hollow trees, the entrance to which is usually a small aperture which must be chopped open to get at the honey.

To the natives in these remote areas honey is a greatly sought-after luxury. It forms a valuable addition to their monotonous diet of maize meal or millet. So you can imagine how honey, one of the most rapidly absorbed forms of energy, can help satisfy a demand, which is almost a craving, for sweet-tasting food.

Because of this Nsulu commands a great respect among the tribes, and much of their folklore and legends centre round the bird, as round any creature which touches the economy of their lives. There are certain rites, too, which must be followed when honey is taken from the hive. It is important for instance to leave a fair portion of the comb for the honey-guide in payment for services rendered. This act must be performed with deference and the appropriate obeisances. And woe betide anyone who neglects this little courtesy. There is no doubt in the minds of these people that such an offender against the proprieties will be adequately punished; the next time he follows Nsulu he will certainly be led into the clutches of a waiting lion or dreaded mamba, or towards any of the other fates that await evil-doers.

The honey-guide is infallible in its purpose. I have never known it fail to find a hive. Of course, sometimes when the hive is opened up you may not find a fresh supply of honey in an edible state but provided the bees are active Nsulu will fulfil his share of the contract by leading you to the hive. In colder northern climates bees are active only in the warmer summer months, but in the tropics honey making continues throughout the year. Perhaps this is the reason for the bad temper which bee-keepers of the world attribute to the African bee.

I remember one day when I was camped in an attractive grove of hyphæne palms in Chikwa's country. It was that in-between period of mid-afternoon when the animals and birds, which had been dozing during the heat of the day, had begun to stir. A slight breeze was rustling the fronds of the palm trees, causing an exaggerated explosive noise as the hollow stems banged together making a loud sound out of all proportion to the slight wind stirring them. Nonetheless it was soothing music, reminding me of my childhood in Chinde when we used to watch the rollers coming from the Indian Ocean and the surf breaking rhythmically on the beautiful golden sand.

Here in Luangwa the palm swifts attracted to this particular palm grove continued to flit tirelessly across the sky without ever appearing to rest. Swifts are some of the most remarkable birds in the world but it is only recently with my newly acquired interest that I have felt a desire to study their habits more closely. Due to the structure of their very long angular wings they are quite incapable of taking off from the ground like, say, a swallow, so that they never settle or roost in the manner of other birds. I suppose that is why palm swifts nest only in tall palm trees, so that they can drop out in a dive and attain flying speed without the risk of becoming entangled with protruding obstacles.

As I watched them I wondered how difficult it would be to climb up and inspect their nests. 'Nest' is not perhaps the best description of the place where these palm swifts lay their eggs. One or sometimes two plain white eggs are stuck to the bare upper surface of the palm frond with adhesive saliva; a few feathers, forming an inadequate cup, are then stuck to the surface, offering little protection for the young when they are hatched. If only I had had a pair of the climbing irons used by maintenance men to climb telegraph poles I might have attempted it. It would have been the only possible way to reach and examine these unique nests.

As it was, I wondered instead whether these palm swifts had the same habits as the all-black European swifts which I used to see during the rainy season flying very high but which, unlike the palm swift, migrate to Europe each spring. Swifts fly at tremendous speeds, faster than any other known bird. Some of them actually sleep on the wing. Nearly two hundred years ago the famous ornithologist Gilbert White recorded the fact that they also mate on the wing, something which has never since been attributed to any other species.

The palm swifts were not the only birds searching for food. As I watched them, an impatient honey-guide came into the camp, chattering persistently. After a burst of twittering to attract attention it moved off to a nearby tree and made one or two short flights in the direction it wanted us to follow. When it saw that nobody was following, it returned, apparently disappointed and frustrated, to start all over again – for all the world like an excited terrier trying to persuade his master to take him for a walk. Even if you are not familiar with the habit of this extraordinary bird there is no mistaking its intentions.

I thought it would be uncharitable to ignore the invitation, so I called one of my carriers, an old man who went by the name of Cabbage and who was considered to be an expert honey collector, and together we started to follow Nsulu. No sooner had we left the precincts of our camp than we were joined by several of our other carriers who wanted to join in the fun. The honey-guide led the lot of us unerringly to a hive nearly two miles away. There was no possible chance of misunderstanding its directions. It simply led us through the woodland from tree to tree, fifteen to twenty yards ahead, keeping up an even chattering noise rather like someone rattling a half-empty box of matches. If we had to deviate in order to avoid a 'donga' (gully) or thorn-patch its chattering would increase in intensity in order to attract us back to the proper course. Words could not have been more eloquent. When ultimately we approached the hive it increased its tempo and became really excited, hovering around the site of the nest in case we should mistake its message. He needn't have worried, for the busy coming and going of the bees and the dark stained aperture which indicated the entrance to the hive twenty feet up the trunk were unmistakable.

Once the hive was located, Cabbage instituted himself as master of ceremonies and immediately sent off one of the others to cut a forked pole to prop against the tree and use as a ladder. While this was being done he borrowed some matches and lit a small fire at the base of the tree. Into this he fed some green fuel to make it smoke profusely. He then collected a piece of dried elephant dung, of which there was plenty near by, and applied a burning ember to it until it smouldered steadily. When the forked pole was in position Cabbage, with an axe over his shoulder, clambered up the trunk with the agility of an aged monkey.

In one hand he carried the smouldering elephant dung, which he placed in a suitable position in a fork of the tree so that the smoke wafted towards the entrance of the hive. Then with deft strokes of his axe he chopped away at the hole while the angry bees buzzed around his head, getting into his hair and stinging his face and neck. Cabbage, oblivious to such trivialities, continued to wield rhythmically his short-handled axe until he had enlarged the hole. He then put his hand and arm in right up to the armpit and searched around in the hollow tree until he came out with a large section of honeycomb dripping with honey. He repeated the performance four times, bringing forth large chunks of honeycomb and dropping them down to his companions below. He was making a messy job of it for his arms and naked chest were covered in honey and bees, but after the few initial stings the swarm seemed to stop their attack on him, particularly since he had adjusted his smoke-screen to blow more directly on to them.

We feasted greedily on the honey, though the Africans prefer those cells which contain the grubs to the pure honey itself. They would fill their mouths with the combs, chew all the nourishment, and then spit out the wax. Meanwhile one of the carriers had cut away a square of bark from a large marula tree; this acted as a sort of gravy boat in which to carry the surplus honey back to camp.

During this operation Nsulu had quietened down, knowing that its part of the operation had been successfully accomplished. But occasionally it reminded us of its presence by a short burst of chattering, just in case we should become too absorbed in our activities to remember our benefactor.

There was a waterhole near by so Cabbage, his task also completed, went along to wash off the sticky mess adhering to various parts of his anatomy. We waited for him a long time before becoming impatient and finally bored. At last we shouted to him to hurry up and follow us and set off for home.

I was sitting down to a peaceful cup of tea in camp when Cabbage returned and asked his companions whether they had left an offering for Nsulu. They said they had not and that it was his responsibility. He abused them roundly, pointing out their doubtful pedigree and inferior tribal status.

There ensued such a heated argument, in which most of the carriers became involved, that I was afraid it might develop into a faction fight. I usually recruited my carriers from Akunda people, but on this trip I had taken some Wisa from Kambwiri's country and these two tribes were traditional enemies. From past experience I realised that such a situation could become volatile. Thinking it time to intervene I called up Cabbage, who was a Wisa, and also the spokesman for the Akunda tribesmen. When we were all seated amicably and the carriers saw their ring-leaders calmly discussing their differences, they dispersed and began to laugh and joke happily among themselves as though such a dispute had never happened.

I then gave Cabbage, who was twice my age, a fatherly lecture on coincidence and the laws of average. I said that it was inevitable that anyone who hunted for honey regularly would occasionally meet up with some dangerous animal. It was impossible to walk in the bush day after day without such an occurrence. When it happened, the person involved would naturally think back and recall some occasion when he had not properly rewarded Nsulu for his services and would immediately associate the two happenings. It was really just coincidence. Could he grasp this? Cabbage thought about it rather dubiously for some time, then grudgingly admitted that the white man had an answer for everything, while his own people interpreted all things as being controlled by magic and ancestral spirits.

But a lifetime of such beliefs is not so easily dispelled and he was not entirely convinced. He said that in spite of my explanation, excellent as it was, he thought he ought to return and leave some honeycomb for Nsulu – just in case. The sun was getting low but he could just make it before dark.

Ten minutes later, priding myself on the tactful manner in

which I had handled a delicate situation, I was sitting down to my interrupted tea when Cabbage came striding back into camp, a look of fury on his wrinkled old face.

He strode up to me pointing his finger accusingly and said in an unpleasantly scathing manner: 'I shall never believe a white man ever again.' Then he proceeded to relate how, after he had left camp, just beyond the combretum scrub he had walked into a sleeping rhino, who had promptly chased him. If it had not been for his prayers to the spirit of his great-uncle, who was known to have special rhino medicine, he would surely have been torn to pieces. What could I say to that?

Honey-guides can be an unmitigated nuisance whilst you are hunting; they will follow you for miles, twittering persistently, pleading with you to follow them. Game animals have come to associate this call with the presence of humans and are immediately warned of the hunter's approach. When you are hot on the spoor it is virtually a waste of time to continue in the presence of a honey-guide. I have often discovered this to my cost.

In addition to making life difficult for hunters honey-guides have another unpleasant habit: they are parasitic, like cuckoos. The mother lays her eggs in the nest of another bird and when the egg hatches out the fledgeling proceeds to murder its host's young with its powerful hooked beak, specially developed for this purpose. It will then kick them over the side of the nest.

Nsulu, then, as you may gather, is a strange creature. He encourages sweetness in others but singularly lacks it in himself.

12. Pathfinders

You cannot live in the bush for long without being made very much aware of the spectacular change that migration brings with it at certain times of the year. This question of seasonal migration has always intrigued me.

For months the whole countryside lies withered and desiccated, thirsty for moisture to quench its parched roots, and then suddenly, at long last, the rains come and the migratory birds seem to filter in. The mopani trees, leafless a few weeks ago, are now cloaked in a delicate shade of apple green and most of the scrub bushes have burst into leaf. A mantle of spring freshness enshrouds the land.

Some of the early migrant birds had been with us for weeks. Yesterday I had watched a flock of white storks which had just arrived on their southward flight from the European winter. Later they would disperse and settle throughout southern Africa. Yet it did not seem so very long since they had left in the opposite direction for the northern spring.

I remember how they gathered in large flocks, spiralling upwards on the thermals till they were mere specks in the sky. They would repeat this performance for several days, as though it were a rallying call for all other white storks to join the excursion to the northern breeding grounds. Then, suddenly, there would be no more white storks in all Africa.

But now they were back again. Life is never dull at this

season, for you are continually renewing acquaintance with avian friends. Until you see or hear a particular bird you do not realise how much you have missed it during its six or seven months sojourn in the north.

A pair of jacobin cuckoos, migrants also, had been calling persistently around my camp during the last week and, although I clearly recognised their call, I had not glimpsed either of them. This was a disappointment to me since I badly wanted to see whether they were black- or white-breasted. For some reason which I have never discovered the same bird appears in two different plumages. They have a black and a white phase. I have only seen them once in the black phase in this country, although it is quite common in South Africa. It is obviously not a breeding plumage, nor even an immature phase, nor, so far as I have been able to gather, is it a result of their geographic environment. Indeed, very little is known of this colour variation, which is described as dimorphism.

These thoughts occupied my mind as I sat watching a pair of common sandpipers feeding along the mudbank on the fringe of the lagoon near my camp at Kapani. As they bobbed their tails and bottoms up and down in characteristic fashion, probing the mud with their beaks, I wondered if they were the same pair I had watched foraging so energetically last season and whose presence I had missed in March when they left for their breeding grounds in Russia. I liked to think they were, for most migrating birds return to the same territory year after year. What a tremendous journey they had just completed, with as little fuss as the number 74 bus doing a routine run between Putney Bridge and Hyde Park Corner.

The legendary journeys of Ulysses, Ghengis Khan and Marco Polo occupy much space in our libraries but, how insignificant their campaigns seem compared with the efforts of these tiny feathered creatures, weighing only a few ounces, who fly halfway round the world twice every year as regularly as the seasons change. How on earth do they accomplish such a journey? Despite recent technical discoveries in the field of electronics, loudly acclaimed by man to prove his godlike mastery over natural processes, we still have nothing to compare with the marvellous navigational equipment that nature has built into some of these small creatures. Nor do we understand it. It is a sobering thought which never fails to instil in me a feeling of awe and humility.

I find comfort in knowing that man has not completely mastered the world. He may be on the brink of conquering space but the tiny sandpiper in front of me, not more than a few inches high, is still able to defy man's computers and is living proof of our inadequacy. If we could only spare a little time from our mundane commitments to ponder just one such example as this, surely it would help us attain a better perspective on the bewildering world in which we live.

What is this marvellous biological mechanism which permits such phenomenal feats of navigation and presents such a challenge to our imagination?

It is known, for instance, that birds navigate by the sun in daytime and by the stars at night, without the need of landmarks. Experiments have been carried out in planetariums with birds showing migratory restlessness. When uncovered in the planetarium they will prepare to take off in the direction they would normally go, depending on the position of the stars. But if the star pattern on the dome is deliberately changed to face the wrong direction, they will orientate themselves towards the false position of the artificial night-sky.

Similar experiments have been conducted to prove that birds fly on a 'sun compass' as well as on a 'star compass'. Such sense of direction of course would be useless unless the navigator knew how far he had travelled along his set course. For this purpose nature has provided birds with a very accurate time sense, a sort of built-in chronometer which allows them to know what distances they have travelled along a certain route. This would be all very well if the sun and stars stayed in one position, but a course taken on the sun, say, at eight o'clock in the morning would be vastly different from a bearing taken in mid-afternoon. Yet, incredible as it seems, their remarkable sense of time is again used to calculate their true course in relation to the position of the sun at any particular time of day. No one knows how this is done; no one has come near to discovering.

The course of birds flying across the sea has been tracked by the most modern radar equipment, and it is shown that they keep a fairly constant heading in fine weather. But, as all air pilots know, however accurately a set bearing is followed there is one factor which will upset his reckoning unless allowance is made for it, and that is 'drift'. You may appear to fly accurately along a set bearing with your nose pointing in the correct direction all the time, but if you encounter a strong cross-wind you will find yourself many miles off course when you reach the end of your journey. An airline pilot receives meteorological reports, which tell him the strength and direction of the winds, and he is able to make the necessary adjustments. A bird cannot do this. That is why birds wait for favourable weather before taking off on a long migratory journey. But in spite of this they often encounter fog and adverse weather conditions.

If they are caught in foggy weather and cannot see the sun or stars, radar-tracking stations show them floundering about hopelessly, drifting on any wind which might arise until they can sight their first landfall. Only when they have landed and recuperated and conditions have once more become favourable are they able to orientate themselves sufficiently to be able to set off for their destination.

No evidence has yet been produced to show that birds are sensitive to magnetic force, so the hidden faculty which enables them to navigate like this is unknown. But it is known that they have some mysterious 'map sense', and once they land they know where they are and can make the adjustments necessary to reach their ultimate destination.

Although for want of a better term I have used the words 'sun compass' and 'star compass' they are not, of course, equipped with anything resembling a magnetic compass nor are they endowed with any 'radar' or echo-sounding faculties similar to those possessed by bats: at least not for navigational purposes. I know of only one exception, the guacharo – a bird which spends most of its life in dark caves in South America. But in this case the device has been evolved so that the bird can find its way about the gloomy world it inhabits.

We are told that migration is an instinctive behaviour and is the product of natural selection. This, of course, does not explain anything: it merely classifies the process and tells us that these feats are inherent and not learnt by experience, which to my mind makes it all the more incredible. Migration, it is said, has evolved because it is of value to the survival of a particular species of bird. Way back in the evolutionary past, birds which had the initiative to move away to more favourable feeding and breeding places survived and produced more progeny than the lazy ones who decided to stay at home. The idle ones faded out. There are certain birds, of course, that are not migratory, so obviously the same theory cannot be applied to all species.

This somewhat inconclusive review of bird migration is not

intended to explain but rather to point out its complexity and to show how little is known of the hidden faculties which make it possible. For example, we cannot account for the fact that many young birds leave their nesting grounds before their parents and undertake the long journey southwards back to their winter home without any guidance from the older experienced birds who have done the journey before.

A classic example of birds finding their way home over unfamiliar territory was demonstrated recently on a small island bird sanctuary off the west coast of Wales (Skokholm). Manx shearwaters, which breed in holes underground on this island, were taken from their nests and transported by air to various destinations, far beyond their normal range, to be released. One bird found its way home from Venice, nearly a thousand miles across Europe; another accomplished the phenomenal feat of returning to its nest from Boston in America, more than three thousand miles across the Atlantic Ocean, completing the journey in twelve and a half days.

We are told that these journeys are not undertaken consciously, that an inborn urge compels them to perform these feats of migration. Experiments have shown that weather, especially temperature, may induce or inhibit the departure of migrants on a journey. Generally speaking, changes in day-length may affect the release of hormones and the condition of reproductive organs, which trigger off this urge to migrate. Other factors, at present little understood, may also be involved. Different species at different seasons in different habitats may be affected by different stimuli. But too little is known on the subject even to guess what the controlling factor is.

We may call it instinct or give it any other name we please, but the whole subject is as incomprehensible as the mystery of life itself. So many unaccountable phenomena in nature are explained away under the guise of 'instinct'. Let them remain so. I personally prefer to believe humbly in a superior force, unknown and unfathomable, one which we are not competent to lay on the dissecting-table or to weigh, measure, analyse or compute.

13. The hunting instinct

Why do people hunt?

I have heard hunting described as 'the unspeakable in pursuit of the uneatable', but to be fair to the hunter this enigma which has puzzled the minds of philosophers for centuries cannot be explained away in a flippant phrase. What is it that compels men to risk their lives hunting dangerous animals in inaccessible places or to expose themselves to the discomforts of tracking down rare creatures through swamp and jungle? One thing you can be sure of: it is not merely the urge to kill, although it cannot be denied that man has inherited a very strong predatory instinct from his pre-human ancestors. Fortunately civilisation has compelled him to inhibit most of these predatory tendencies. But they are still there in all of us, and it would be foolish, perhaps dangerous, to forget it.

The higher an animal ascends in the evolutionary ladder the less dependent it becomes upon instinct for survival and the more it relies upon a system of learnt behaviour, among men upon a code of ethics. This behaviour has to be learned anew by each succeeding generation but the primordial predatory urges are never entirely eliminated; there is always a subconscious conflict between the two.

Regardless of how we rationalise this hunting urge there is no doubt that a true sportsman will go to endless trouble, and perhaps save up for a lifetime, in order to afford a trip to Africa to shoot a buffalo. If you were to suggest that he could satisfy this urge equally well and at considerably less expense by shooting a cow on a neighbour's farm he would be horrified. For, of course, he does not want to *kill* a buffalo; he wants to *hunt* it. He seeks adventure and excitement – and the thousand other emotions which contribute to the magic of a safari in Africa. The greater his privation and danger the greater will be his satisfaction and sense of achievement.

There are, of course, other reasons why people hunt. But let us consider the typical hunter. He seeks adventure. He takes up a challenge compelled by the same inherent call which drove Sir Edmund Hillary upward more than twenty-nine thousand feet to the summit of Everest: the same urge which spurred Robert Peary to endure extreme discomfort, plodding through limitless snowy wastes, many degrees below zero, in order to be the first man to reach the North Pole. This indomitable spirit did not die with the national heroes of the past; it is constantly with us. Nor does it diminish with the flush of youth. As I write, a courageous, ageing man, with very few years remaining to reach the prescribed three score and ten, is alone in a small sailing boat in the middle of the South Atlantic, having successfully conquered tempestuous seas on the first stage of his journey round the world. His name: Francis Chichester. Of such material is our evolution built.

The opponents of hunting will say that these particular examples do not support my argument because this type of adventurer does not take life; but the fundamental reason in both cases is the same. It is a response to a challenge, to prove to the world, but more importantly to oneself, that one can do something better than one's neighbour. The adventurer wants to convince himself of his superiority in whatever field he chooses to express himself, whether as sportsman, musician, artist or explorer. In one respect these vocations are all alike. They form an arena in which man can test his own strength.

Without this testing, this constant striving to do better than other people, our civilisation would collapse. It is the basis of our society. Even the lowest forms of life compete with one another for food and space in the continual struggle for survival. It is only the successful ones in this competitive struggle, those with aggressiveness and the urge to dominate and excel, who survive and pass on to their progeny their superior attainments, thereby keeping the species healthy and virile.

To deny the need for effort and improvement, to opt out of the struggle, is the first step towards neurosis and decadence. We may not all want to hunt but we cannot afford to under-rate the influence of instinct in our everyday life.

Perhaps its inexorable trend can best and most graphically be explained by the oft-quoted example of the European beaver. Several hundred years ago beavers in Europe were reduced so drastically that they ceased to perform their age-old custom of building dams and lodges and it was thought that they had lost the art of these communal labour projects. (The custom continued as usual among the thriving colonies of beavers in Canada.) The French Government, fearing the extermination of the beaver, gave sanctuary to a remnant of these industrious little animals in the Rhône River. Here the European beavers multiplied and thrived, and when the population reached the optimum number they started up their communal activities strictly according to the age-old beaver tradition: this, after a lapse of several hundred years. The dams and lodges they constructed were identical in every respect to those built by their relatives across the Atlantic. Although the circumstances favourable to their constructional habits had been absent for a number of centuries the instinct still remained unimpaired, ready to be revived when the population became large enough to trigger it off.

Robert Ardrey in his fascinating book *African Genesis* unfolds dramatically and convincingly the theory of how present-day man evolved from a species of carnivorous ape which existed in Africa in the early Pleistocene era. The theory is not his: he takes up the cudgels on behalf of Professor Raymond Dart.

Ardrey is not a professional scientist, he is a dramatist, and he has treated a highly technical subject in a most readable and often humorous manner so convincingly that a layman reading his words could scarcely doubt that his ancestor, three-quarters of a million years ago and long before the appearance of the first *Homo sapiens*, was a predatory ape who sallied from his cave armed with a bone club to slay his prey.

Before Professor Dart's finds in the fossil beds in Makapan, two hundred miles north of Johannesburg, it was almost universally believed that man originated in Asia and descended from a herbivorous ape-like animal somewhat similar to the primates living today. Tools or weapons, it was believed, came into use after true man came on the scene: in fact, *after* he began to develop a degree of intelligence and an enlarged brain cavity.

Dart set out to explode this universally accepted view of man's origin, much to the chagrin of the orthodox scientists of the world. Rather unsportingly Dart showed that Africa and not Asia was the cradle of mankind. The skull he discovered had a small brain cavity and belonged to an animal who walked erect and preceded, by 250,000 years, the Pekin Man (*Pithecan-thropus erectus*) and all other sub-humans ever unearthed. He named his discovery *Australopithecus africanus*, which means 'the South African ape'. Furthermore, among the thousands of fossil remains which he examined he noticed numerous skulls from an early type of baboon, all of which had obviously received similar fatal head injuries. Continuing his excavations and accumulating material over many years, he built up evidence showing that it was this ape-man who first used weapons with which to slaughter his prey. By classifying more than 4,000 fossil remains he found that an overwhelming proportion consisted of the humerus (upper front leg-bone and knuckle) of a medium-sized antelope, which was obviously used as a club. By the same method he proved the use of other weapons or tools. The knuckle-bone of the humerus in nearly every case fitted perfectly the indentations in the smashed cranium of the fossilised baboon skulls.

From this evidence he concluded that man's predecessors originated in Central Africa, that he was a predator, and that weapons were used by sub-humans with a small brain long before the advent of true man.

For many years Dart's theory was ridiculed by the scientific world, principally on the ground that his first *Australopithecus* skull, on which he based his theory, was that of an immature animal. Since that time, however, many skulls from mature creatures have been found and such an eminent scientist as Professor Broom, working independently on the valuable fossil material from the Sterkfontein caves near Johannesburg, has come to his support. Meanwhile two thousand miles northwards, near the equator, Dr. J. S. B. Leakey is unearthing a fantastic quantity of implements used by an even earlier type of sub-human in the Olduvai Gorge area, which will without doubt add further support to the theory of man's origins in Africa.

But what connection, you will say, have all these dusty

lime-encrusted fossils with the opening question in this chapter? Why does man hunt?

I have tried to show that early man was a hunter, that contemporary man has inherited this instinct, that instincts passed down from our ancestors are ineradicable even though civilisation compels us to inhibit them, that the will to dominate – which implies aggression and hostility – is an even more ancient instinct going back millions of years and is one of the most important factors in evolution. This urge to dominate often finds expression in adventurous pursuits, particularly hunting, which is an instinct we have inherited from that unpronounceable bloke called *Australopithecus*.

However we may try to rationalise it, the urge remains. However we may try to moralise about it, we must face the fact that instincts can be successfully channelled but not denied. We are as we are and however we try to improve we can only do so by disciplining the basic elements within us, not by pretending they do not exist. We belong to the order of nature, and hunting is of that order.

This is not to insist we should all do it or enjoy it, though many of us do, but that we should understand it and recognise and respect its demands. My own personal attitude towards hunting is more expedient. I learnt to hunt before I learnt to think and certainly before others had thought of telling me that to do so was immoral and absurd. For years I loved it but, while still recognising the thrill of the chase, I gave up hunting just for thrills many years ago. I have had my fill and have more or less come to terms with myself on that score. I no longer have to prove to myself that I am unafraid when I face a wounded lion. I *know* I am afraid. But I have proved to my own satisfaction that I can cope with such an emergency should it arise.

14. Safaris

However one may rationalise the hunting instinct my own participation in hunting safaris has given me considerable qualms from time to time. I have often wondered how a High Court judge must feel when he passes capital sentence. But it is not always from the seclusion of my conscience or from the elevated position of the bench that I have had to state my case.

As a professed animal lover I have, on many occasions, been put on trial by my anti-blood-sport friends for my role in organising these hunting safaris. And I have often found it difficult to justify to them my attitude. I try to explain that I am primarily a conservationist and that, although I love individual animals, I am more concerned about the survival of the species as a whole or, better still, the community of species which make up a particular habitat. I tell them that it is sometimes necessary to be cruel to an individual animal in order to protect the lives of the countless other creatures in the community. Sometimes it is essential to kill off surplus animals in order to preserve the sanctuary which was created for their protection and which, if incorrectly managed, would result in the death of not just the few individuals, but of the whole population.

It is therefore true to say that, in a sense, the habitat is far more important than the animals themselves. If there is enough food, shelter, dispersal ground, trace elements in the soil and dozens of other factors which make up the complete habitat, then a healthy population is assured, but once the range becomes degraded by over-stocking or for any other reason, the animals will be unable to exist. They will die and all the care in the world will not bring them back.

I have gone into these factors at some length in a later chapter. Both over-population and danger to habitat provide arguments in support of culling. But I suppose my real justification is based, if not upon the need for culling, then upon that other equally good conservation principle: the economic utilisation of wildlife as part of a land usage plan.

The days are past, especially in Africa, when large tracts of undeveloped land can be set aside as game sanctuaries purely for sentimental or aesthetic reasons. In view of the human population explosion and the clamour to reclaim more and more land, it has become imperative that the natural resources should be fully harnessed and developed; otherwise the land will be entirely usurped for purposes which could be inimical to the animals.

It was precisely because Peter Hankin and I were prepared both to look after the best interests of the wildlife and to develop its economic potential that we were granted a large hunting concession in the Luangwa Valley in which to organise our safaris. This is an extensive area which embraces virtually the entire Valley, excluding the game reserves, and is one of the best stocked game areas it is possible to find in Africa.

Peter is among the top professional hunters in the business today, and I could not have chosen a finer partner. Strangely enough, my earliest contact with him was as an opponent many years previously. It is a curious coincidence that we should later become close friends and business partners.

Our first association took place just before the war, when I was working as an elephant control officer. Although I was employed principally as an elephant hunter, one of my sub-sidiary tasks was to enforce the game laws. During my wander-ings I heard a great deal about a certain Bwana Chiduli who had been just ahead of me in many of the places I visited. Bwana Chiduli was an ivory poacher. On several occasions miles away in the bush I would come across the bleached bones and skull of an elephant and when I inquired from the local natives I would learn that it had been shot by Bwana Chiduli. He was a mythical figure who would suddenly appear out of the blue with only sufficient porters to carry the minimum of food and his ill-gained tusks. He would shoot an elephant and disappear the same day.

I always assumed that he must have hidden his tusks, return-ing later to collect them, but I was never able to find these caches although I interrogated the villagers thoroughly. According to local reputation he was a crack shot and of course most popular with the villagers because of the meat he provided. Perhaps this is why they were reluctant to give me any helpful information. When he appeared in a village, complete with tusks, he would tell the people where to go to cut up the meat. He would never stay long or camp near a village but would always press on to some unknown destination. I am not sure how he acquired his name: *Chiduli* means 'short cut'. Perhaps it was because he never kept to the paths when he was travel-ling. Any such association in the name was, I feel sure, purely terrestrial and had no cynical allusion to his habit of by-passing the game laws.

One day I came to a village and learnt that he had been there two days before, so I decided to pursue him and apprehend him for poaching. I left the bulk of my equipment and travelling light with only a few carriers I covered twenty-five to thirty miles a day on his tracks for the next two weeks. Although I followed many false trails and was on the point of catching up with him on several occasions, he always seemed to manage to be one or two bounds ahead.

It was a long time before I was to find out the identity of this elusive poacher. In fact it was three years later, in the Officers' Club in Addis Ababa, that I first met Bwana Chiduli himself.

Among the party at the bar was a fair haired artillery officer. Whenever you meet anyone from a foreign country in Africa you exchange introductions, discuss your respective places of domicile and search around conversationally for mutual acquaintances. I soon learnt that this stranger was from Northern Rhodesia, and furthermore that he knew the Luangwa Valley intimately. I became interested and it was not long before I had discovered that Captain Hankin and Bwana Chiduli were one and the same person.

We had many drinks to celebrate our long postponed meeting, although it was a far cry from the days when we used to play cops and robbers in the Luangwa Valley. We reminisced happily into the night, pausing only to complain about how tame the war seemed compared to elephant-hunting in our Valley.

During the time I have been associated with hunting safaris, I have made many friends and met some very unusual people. I have also shared many exciting experiences with clients. But it is not the dramatic events one remembers so much as the interesting colourful characters involved.

One safari in particular will always remain in my memory. We had a very flamboyant American couple hunting with us who liked to be known as Jungle Jim and Diamond Nell. Nell glittered with jewellery and Jim did his best to live up to his past by wearing a leopard skin band around his eight-gallon hat and a six-shooter and hunting knife girdled round his waist. They were good church-going people from a Quaker family in the mid-West and were strict teetotallers. Much to our surprise, Jungle Jim was an excellent shot who succeeded in securing a creditable collection of trophies.

Unfortunately, Fritz and Jake elected to come on the same safari. Fritz was a notorious lawyer and Jake was his client from the underworld of Chicago whom he had successfully defended in a recent court case. Jake was not the slightest bit interested in hunting and I could not help surmising that he had undertaken this rather expensive safari not for hunting but for health reasons: it was probably healthier for him to be away from his home town until the storm subsided.

Needless to say, the two parties had little in common except their domicile. Never was there a stricter segregation in camp until their enforced get-together each evening at meal time. Jake had the most valuable set of gold teeth I have seen in any mouth. When he smiled it reminded me of a flash of lightning. We gave him the nick-name 'Sunshine', which pleased him vastly. In spite of his dubious past, perhaps because of it, he was a most entertaining character, keeping us amused with a fund of stories about borderline activities in his city.

It is the custom when people first arrive on a hunting safari to brief them thoroughly about the game laws and, particularly when they are newcomers to Africa, to give them some idea about the methods of hunting the animals they are likely to encounter. Although rather tedious, this briefing is very necessary if you want to avoid any misunderstandings later on safari.

On this occasion it was Peter, a meticulous chap, who was holding the floor. Jake was obviously becoming less and less interested as the lesson progressed. When he could stand it no longer he called out: 'Listen, Peter, why don't you cut out all this crap. You just set 'em up and we'll mow 'em down!'

During this safari Herbert Riseley was managing the domestic side of camp, while Peter Hankin and I concentrated on the actual hunting. Peter took out Jungle Jim and I hunted with Fritz. Jake usually stayed in camp drinking beer and reading Westerns.

There was every incitement to stay behind as the camp was built on an attractive stretch of the river in the shade of a grove of evergreen trichelia, which grow in profusion in this area and provide welcome shade during the heat of the day. Although the camp was made of poles and thatch it was equipped with fridges and spring beds and we even improvised hot and cold showers. Altogether it provided most of the essential comforts expected nowadays without spoiling the bush atmosphere which clients so much enjoyed.

Unfortunately this type of camp has to be rebuilt, or at least refurbished, each season. For when the sites are unoccupied during the rains the elephants take over their rightful domain and indulge in the mischievous habit of tearing down the walls and roofs. When next you visit them you find the dining-shelter poles mixed up with the bedroom thatch and everything scattered far and wide. A few days' work at the beginning of each season with a gang of boys, however, soon repairs the damage.

Such was our camp at Salimu when Herbert went down to prepare it a few days before the arrival of Jungle Jim's party. One evening, just before they were due, Herbert was relaxing in the dining-shelter after a busy day of reconstruction. The camp was illuminated by a pressure lamp hanging from a pole in the shelter and the bull frogs were croaking loudly. For reasons of his own Herbert got up to leave the room. On both going out and coming back he had to walk in front of the lamp. On both occasions he automatically blocked the light from the water and the frogs stopped croaking.

This was too good to be true. He tried again – longer this time – and again it worked. Every time the result was the same; when the light was blocked the frogs were silent. This was too good a discovery to keep to himself. Herbert was a great one for practical jokes. He decided he would make capital out of the situation as soon as our guests arrived.

The following evening, when Jungle Jim's party had arrived in camp and the frogs were particularly vociferous, Herbert steered the conversation round to witchcraft and black magic. He did it slowly and skilfully, lying back in his chair confident and at ease. The story he told them covered a long stretch of his youth, spent hunting in Mozambique. He told how he had once been lucky enough to shoot a buffalo which had killed the nephew of an Anguru chief. The story became more involved; he settled back more comfortably to tell it.

This Chief's family belonged, he explained, to the frog totem and he and certain chosen members of the clan were able to talk to the frogs, which were considered to be sacred. As a reward for his services in shooting the rogue buffalo, the Chief had made Herbert an honorary member of the clan and had given him some frog 'muti' (medicine).

Herbert was a practised story-teller and by this time had the undivided attention of all our guests. Peter and I had already been treated to a rehearsal some days previously and knew what to expect, but in order to back him up we pretended to be sceptical and challenged him to prove his magical powers.

Herbert went to his hut, collected a few pieces of rubbish and with great ceremony began reciting some mumbo-jumbo while walking towards the front of the shelter where the lamp was

hanging. Meanwhile the frogs were croaking loudly. When he
had achieved a sufficiently dramatic atmosphere he stepped in
front of the lights and effectively lifted his hand as though he
were Canute holding back the waves, 'Tontola!' ('Shut up!'),
he shouted.

There was an absolute and deathly silence: not a frog was to
be heard. Herbert held this theatrical pose for probably ten
seconds, then, in a calmer voice, shouted 'Chabwino, yimbani!'
('All right, carry on.') As he moved away from the lamp the
frogs started up, slowly at first and then gradually increasing
their tempo until they were croaking again as loudly as before.
But the guests still sat without speaking, uncertain how to cope
with such supernatural prowess. They never cottoned on.

ENLIGHTENMENT

15. Trails in the wilderness

Not so many years ago I inaugurated a non-shooting type of safari with a difference, which I called a 'wilderness trail'. It is virtually a walking tour in the game reserve, miles away from habitation or man-made tracks, with a trail of porters carrying one's requirements in the traditional African manner; in fact little changed from the methods of Livingstone and Stanley.

Such a safari always brings back to me nostalgic memories of earlier times when the only means of transport was on foot. It helps to recall, too, a sense of completeness, of peaceful unity with nature, and to conjure up idyllic scenes of animals grazing undisturbed in peaceful riverine glades, where there is always time to pause and study their uninhibited actions without any feelings of guilt because you are wasting somebody else's time.

Time nowadays is a commodity that increases in value with each succeeding year. Every hour not spent rushing from one place to another seems to be a debit entry which will have to be accounted for on the Day of Reckoning. Time was invented by man and he has now made himself a slave to it. It is a pity, for it is impossible, travelling at thirty miles an hour, to get to know an area intimately and to reflect on the intricate relationship between the soils, the vegetation and the fauna.

Africa has now been opened up to the four-wheel-drive vehicle and a journey that used to take a month can now be accomplished in a day or so. Very little touring on foot is undertaken any more, even by field officers, who now take Unimogs and Halflingers into areas too rough even for Land Rovers – horrible, dinky-toy contraptions consisting of a platform on wheels propelled by noisy, smelly engines from which every animal flees on sight.

How peaceful and revealing it is by contrast to sit in camp at the end of a day's trek and watch, for example, a pair of white-headed plovers sharing their nesting duties. Their nest is a mere depression in the sandy river bed – I think perhaps a 'scrape' is a better description – and they make no attempt to embellish it. The four cryptic buff-coloured eggs are cunningly camouflaged and practically impossible to see against the background of sand and stones which the bird has selected as its nesting site. If anyone should approach, the plover will cheep and twitter hysterically, sometimes even dive-bomb you and then fly off to a patch of beach some distance off, performing all kinds of peculiar antics in order to divert your attention from the nest. How can you possibly enjoy these little domestic displays from the seat of a motor-car?

Then again, to talk around the camp fire to men who have now become individuals rather than a line of porters carrying their burdens is an experience in itself. For any one of them has a lifetime of knowledge and anecdotes which he is only too ready to impart. How else can you get to know the intriguing customs and traditions of these simple natural people, or listen to their stories about the wild creatures which they know so well? How else unravel the apparently inextricable confusion between their own astute observations and their naïve acceptance of folklore?

It is to these trails that I look back with greatest pleasure. They are difficult to recapture exactly, but I would like to give others an opportunity to savour something of the excitement, the glamour and the atmosphere of Africa as it used to be.

On this sort of safari I like to restrict my guests to four, for it is difficult for one leader to look after more than this number without the party becoming a crowd. Usually we break camp early in the morning, for that is the time when the animals are most active. You might catch sight of some of the night prowlers returning late to their hideout – a honey badger, a hyena, or even a lion before he settles down in the shade to laze away the heat-laden hours until the sun's slanting rays become cool enough for him once again to pad his haughty way along the forest tracks.

Your walking pace is leisurely, interspersed with halts to observe the animals. Your carriers are far behind, for you left them to pack up camp while your own small advance party went on ahead; they will catch up later when it is time to look round for a site to pitch the tents at the end of your morning trek. Your path is not always the most direct one, for you will have to make many detours to avoid animals – the ones, that is, who have right of way. This is an arbitrary right but one it is safer not to ignore. You can interpret it simply by giving way to those animals with whom you would rather not have a showdown. You would be wiser, for instance, not to dispute the right of way with a herd of elephants across your path, intent on minding their own elephantine business. Merely test the wind and give them a wide berth, especially if there are any cows and calves in the herd, making sure that the wind is blowing directly from them to you. After you have made a wide detour and feel confident that you have out-flanked the herd, you may easily discover a stray group in the bushes ahead that you have not taken into account. You may then have to retreat and make an even wider encircling movement. And so it goes on: all morning you are either watching, stalking, or avoiding some intriguing tableau on this outdoor stage.

By midday you are encamped, probably in the shade of some evergreen trees on the sheer bank of the river, with a grandstand view of a school of hippo doing nothing more onerous than passing the time. Even this can be tiring without some assistance, so the hippos enlist one another's help by resting their heavy heads on their neighbour's flank.

All other creatures in the Valley seem to be dozing away those midday hours; perhaps you begin to think that they have a point, and before you know where you are the boy is waking you up for tea that precedes the afternoon walk.

The companionship of a camp fire, the smell of mopane smoke, and the talk of shared adventures against a backdrop of African night noises is an atmosphere difficult to simulate, but once you have experienced it you are near to finding infinite contentment. It is always with regret that a guest finds himself back at Mfuwe at the end of a Wilderness Trail.

A certain French Consul in Southern Africa, whom I will call Monsieur Marchet, was one of our most enthusiastic clients. He was rotund and cheerful and what little hair he had was cropped short. We called him Jean. He had a battery of cine cameras and other paraphernalia with which to record his enthusiasm and when I met him at the airport I knew at once that he would be an amusing companion during the next seven days. His eyes twinkled with merriment as he spoke to us in his attractive French accent. He classed himself as a diplomat, and a diplomat, he confided to me, was a person who could say nothing in seventeen different languages.

On the second day out we had pitched camp at a beautiful spot among a grove of tall shady Mbawa trees (*Kia niasicca*) on the bank of the Kapamba River, with clear crystal water flowing between the sandbanks. None of us could resist the enticingly cool water after our walk in the heat of the day. As we were an all-bachelor party any form of modesty would have been fastidious, so we bathed as nature intended. To see Jean sporting himself in the water like a white hippo seemed so delightfully incongruous that I could not resist the temptation to put it on record. Stretching out for his Bolex cine camera, I shot off about 15 feet of film through the telephoto lens without his being aware of it.

A couple of weeks later I received an enthusiastic letter from him in Salisbury, saying how much he had enjoyed his safari and how greatly he was looking forward to seeing the results of his films; they had been processed but he had not yet had time to project them. However, he added by way of postscript, he would see them in the next twenty-four hours as he had been asked to show them at a reception the following day at the Embassy in honour of a visiting German ambassador.

The following Christmas I received a card from him from the Chad territory. My conscience has worried me ever since. And it is all too easy to picture his intense embarrassment when, at a formal ambassadorial evening, a pastoral shot of grazing zebra was rudely shattered by a strip-tease act. It would be difficult to explain away: even in seventeen different languages. It is dreadful to think that what was simply intended as an innocent prank might have caused him to be posted to a hell station in the Sahara desert.

My following trip gave me an unusual companion in the form of an attractive American woman, Cecelia, with her son and nephew, both about 11 or 12 years old. Cecelia was a proud mother and for the benefit of the boys had courageously undertaken this trip on the other side of the world which she had heard about through a travel agent in Los Angeles. I am pleased to think that she enjoyed the adventure even more than they did.

As they were the only clients booked on this safari I invited Peter Tolson to come along as a guest to complete the party. I had recently met Peter and was at once attracted to this reserved but friendly Englishman. He was a well-known ornithologist and was making a detailed study of the birds of the Valley. Peter was the most enthusiastic bird-watcher I have ever met. At first I was identifying birds for him but although he had been in Africa only a few weeks, it was not long before he was teaching me.

I have a passing knowledge of the local birds but when it comes to the warblers and cisticolas, all drab brown and practically impossible to tell apart, I give up trying to identify them. Peter on the other hand was a fanatic and would not be satisfied until he had put a name to every bird he saw. All day long he could be seen peering into bushes or trees through his binoculars. When he lowered them he would have that faraway look in his eyes peculiar to a certain breed of nature lover. Then he would mumble some ornithological jargon to himself, reach into his haversack for one of his reference books, and track down his victim's identity. Most ornithologists are crazy anyway.

During our trek through the bush I would give up waiting for him and go ahead with Cecelia and the two boys, while he remained behind with a guide gazing at an emerald-spotted wood-dove or some other member of the avifauna. Every now and then he would catch up with us, because we halted fairly frequently to take photographs or watch the animals. When he managed to add another bird to his list he became as excited as a schoolboy with his first bicycle.

The author with his two foster cubs, Big Boy and Little Boy

(Overleaf) A lioness chases a vulture off her kill.
Eventually, when she has had her fill, she will go off
to water leaving the field open to the scavengers

The author, his two foster children, and their territory

One dramatic moment occurred on the fourth day out when I was leading with Cecelia, the boys following close behind. We were walking along the river-bank in fairly open country among scattered combretum bushes and trees when I saw some way ahead a small herd of elephant cows and calves advancing upon us. They were quite unaware of us as the wind was blowing obliquely across front, but they were advancing at a fair pace. I hurriedly shepherded my charges into the shelter of a mopani tree thirty-odd yards to the left, hoping this would give sufficient cover and leave enough room for the herd to pass between us and the river. The herd, however, had spread out and it looked as though they would come too close for safety. Peter was not with us; I had no time to worry about him and assumed he was safely bird-watching. I was standing on guard with my rifle loaded and the safety-catch off, undecided whether to fire a shot over their heads, or scare them off by going into the open and waving my arms and shouting at them, when the wind suddenly veered round and the elephants caught our scent, turned tail and went stampeding off, squealing and trumpeting loudly in a terrified manner.

I breathed a sigh of relief and was inwardly congratulating myself on getting out of the scrape without having to fire a shot, when Peter came rushing up to me breathlessly and said: 'Norman, did you see that?' 'Of course I bloody well saw it,' I replied rather brusquely. I was hurt that he had not appreciated the efficient and composed manner in which I had dealt with the emergency.

'But it had white edges to its primary feathers!' he said in a tone of deep resentment. He had been peering through his binoculars at a red-billed hoopoe, totally oblivious to our drama which he had missed completely.

16. Foster-children

My interest in animals was not entirely confined to wild ones. One of the most rewarding experiences I ever had was with two pet lions. The full story of how I fostered these lions from tiny cubs, eventually returning them to their own environment after four years, has already been told in my book *Return to the Wild*. When the book was reviewed a well-known critic writing in a London newspaper described it as 'an interesting story told by two lions about a man'. Having no literary lions to whom I can delegate the present assignment let me, as a mere human, recall some of the experiences we enjoyed together six years ago.

There is nothing very novel about raising lions; many people in Africa have done so – in fact one of the surest means of achieving notoriety is to be the owner of a lion. But in most cases, when the lion begins to grow up and is big enough to gobble up little Johnny, he is banished to a circus or zoo. This usually takes place (I mean the banishment, not the gobbling up) after the lion is twelve months old and his unpredictable and boisterous behaviour makes him a danger to the community. After one year lions grow rapidly and at two years they are fully matured and should really be kept behind bars if they are to be on display. Surprising as it may seem, when a lion has been reared as a pet he is quite unable to fend for himself in the wild. He possesses an inherent instinct to hunt together with

the inability to put this instinct into practice. If he were released in a game reserve he would starve to death.

In the wild state a lioness teaches her cubs how to hunt and
kill their prey. This is a very thorough and protracted training,
starting when they are only a few weeks old and continuing
until they graduate to full maturity two years later. Without
this instruction they are ill-equipped to hold their own in the
tough, severely competitive world of their elders.

How I taught my lions to hunt and fend for themselves, and
how I released them as fully competent animals, was the main
theme of *Return to the Wild*. A year after their release in a
remote part of the Northern Luangwa Valley Game Reserve I
again made contact with them and found that they had overcome the handicap of their artificial upbringing and were well
established in their new territory.

I adopted these lions in 1957 when I was Warden of the
Kafue National Park. One of my African Game Guards was on
patrol when his path crossed that of an irate lioness. Thinking
her cubs were endangered, she immediately attacked the Game
Guard who in self-defence was forced to shoot her. It was only
afterwards that he discovered she had cubs, so he brought them
to me to adopt or – to put it more accurately – for them to
adopt me.

So began the most interesting and fascinating association
with animals that I have ever experienced. For the next four
years my foster-father duties took up a great deal of my time.
While the cubs were young these parental duties were shared;
they were adorable creatures and my Game Rangers were only
too pleased to baby-sit if necessary. It would have been impossible otherwise to get away from headquarters and attend to
the numerous duties which required my attention in the
National Park.

I adopted the cubs when they were two tiny balls of fur only a week old, and they acquired the names of Big Boy and Little Boy very early in life. Not that there was very much difference in their appearance but Big Boy was always the leader and easily assumed the role of big brother. In their characters, however, they were as different as brothers can be; Big Boy was placid and easy-going, whereas Little Boy was temperamental and sometimes very difficult to handle.

During their first year they remained in our main camp at Ngoma in the National Park and gave considerable pleasure to the large number of visitors, who loved to pet them and have their photographs taken with them. The cubs were rather rough, even at that age, and were always ready to use their dew claws, which is the lion equivalent of our thumb, to cling on to clothing or flesh. Several torn shirts or dresses, or even sometimes a bloody flesh-wound, were left behind as a memento of these encounters. But there were few complaints. It was surprising how proud a visitor could be of his battle scars.

In their second year, the cubs were too dangerous to be left free among visitors. They had to be banished to a remote part of the Park. This presented problems because I had to go out every second or third day to feed them. Very soon they began to associate the sound of a motor-car, particularly a Land-Rover, with feeding-time and whenever they were hungry and heard the distant sound of an engine they would get the urge to wander and eventually find their way back to camp. Some of their terrifying adventures with wild lions and their mischievous encounters with tourists I have already related elsewhere. They were, in fact, a far greater danger to the public than wild lions, for whereas a wild lion has a healthy respect for man and will not approach too close, my lions did not fear man at all: on the contrary they enjoyed the association and would deliberately seek him out. This resulted in many complications, especially when a visitor met one of them and did not realise he was tame.

I was beginning to worry about their future when providence stepped in and provided a solution. My assignment as Warden of the National Park was coming to an end; I had fulfilled my purpose in getting the Park developed and it was now running smoothly for the second year, catering to a regular flow of tourists. It was at this juncture that I was offered a freelance job to make a wildlife survey of the Luangwa Valley. I would take my lions with me.

I had immediate visions of my foster-children growing up wild and uninhibited in their new surroundings where I could teach them to hunt without any extraneous influences interrupting their training. And this is in fact what happened. Up to now I had been bound to my headquarters at Ngoma, where there were three European families and a large African staff, but in my new job I would be able to operate from whatever base I cared to choose and as remote as I wished. I did not hesitate to accept the new post.

When I left the Kafue National Park I took with me my faithful Game Guard, Nelson, who had helped me to bring up the lions. We had a wire-mesh frame fitted over the rear of my Land-Rover and, with the lions securely inside, the four of us travelled non-stop to the Luangwa Valley seven hundred miles away. We established camp on the banks of the Luangwa River, far away from any human beings, and this became the setting for many adventures during the next two years.

I called my camp Kapani, which is the native name for a nearby lagoon. It was delightful to be back in my old stamping ground again, an area which I knew so well. The lions, too, seemed to love their free-roaming, unrestricted home for they were not enclosed or confined in any way and were free to come and go as they wished. At first they kept close to my grass shack but later, when they became more familiar with their new territory, they would wander further and further afield and sleep on the cool sandy beach in front of the camp. Later, when they were more proficient in hunting, they would go off for several days at a time.

I had no set plan for training the lions to hunt: it was mainly a question of trial and error. As I have said, the instinct to hunt is inborn and it was a matter of encouraging rather than teaching them. From early cubhood they could never resist chasing anybody or anything that ran, so it was a natural step to encourage them to chase the fleeing animals which were so plentiful around Kapani. During the heat of the day, like their wild brothers, they were reluctant to move from the shady spot they had selected, but in the early morning or late afternoon they liked to accompany me on a walk. During these walks I would attempt to manœuvre them, under cover, on the downwind side of a grazing herd of waterbuck or other game, and when we surprised a herd at close quarters Big Boy and Little Boy would automatically give chase.

At first this was just a game and they never really made any serious attempt to catch up with their quarry when it galloped off so much faster than they could hope to follow. But as Nelson and I were feeding them once or twice a week with replicas of the animals they chased, they gradually began to associate the two. Besides, from the scent, the most highly developed sense in wild animals, there could be no doubt of the connection between the animals they were pursuing and their dinner.

Whenever they were presented with a whole carcass they would attack it savagely, growling and demonstrating just like any wild lion who has made the kill himself. There was no doubt in my mind that they would eventually attack a live animal in just the same way when the opportunity arrived. But lions are inordinately lazy creatures and as long as we fed them, why should they bother to exert themselves?

It was inevitable though that one day, with the wind in the right direction, they would come across some unsuspecting animal and make a kill. This is what we hoped for and this is what happened. They made their first kill by chance and from then on their kills became more and more frequent until eventually they were killing regularly for themselves once or twice a week.

Knowing they would never have that driving urge-to-kill which is stimulated only by hunger, I deliberately kept them hungry, feeding them just enough to keep them from starving but hungry enough to urge them to seek their own food. The whole training process was very gradual, but eventually they graduated and were ready to be taken to their new home where I intended to abandon them and leave them to their own resources. I had previously reconnoitred a suitable wilderness area miles away in the northern game reserve.

Before I could do this, however, I had agreed to let them be filmed by the Government Film Unit. The Film Unit, which at my insistence had been kept to a bare minimum, consisted of Anker Atkinson (the Director), and his cameraman, Roger Fairley. Liz (Anker Atkinson's wife), who, incidentally, was also Roger's sister, acted as continuity-girl and made up the family team.

We worked hard together for the next six weeks, although our camera team were at first rather apprehensive about sharing the camp with two lions who were not always pre-dictable with strangers. In the beginning, Nelson and I found it difficult to relax, as our attention was constantly divided between our own affairs and the safety of our guests. It was not beyond the bounds of possibility that the lions would become frivolous and give one of the visitors a playful swipe, so we had to know where everybody was all the time. After the first week the lions accepted the strangers as part of our pride but nonetheless we could not afford to relax our vigil entirely.

We had innumerable difficulties to start with in getting our production under way, not least of which was the temperamental attitude of our stars; a common practice, I am told, on film locations all over the world. But while Hollywood had the advantage over us in that its actors and actresses are bound by certain conditions laid down in their contract, my lions, lacking such constraint, would deliberately absent themselves from work for several days at a time. The whole production would then grind to a halt while Nelson and I desperately searched the surrounding country for the missing truants.

Luckily, our patience was amply rewarded in the end by the first-class film the team made. After treatment by the backroom boys in the studios in Salisbury it was considered good enough to be released on the cinema circuits throughout the world under the title *Return to the Wild*.

The plot was simple and uncomplicated and little was demanded of Nelson and myself in the way of acting. We merely continued living our normal lives with the lions while the cameras followed our actions. A perfect setting surrounded us and our 'extras' were the wild animals which abound in this part of the Valley. We did, however, introduce one extraneous character and that was 'Charlie'.

I caught Charlie the day after the film unit arrived and kept him in a sack. Charlie was a python and it was our intention to use him as a 'prop' in one of the scenes. He was a good-natured snake and when he was not curled up in the sack I would let him out for exercise in the camp. Unhappily, Liz (our continuity-girl) was not partial to Charlie. Big Boy and Little Boy liked him even less. But everyone else got on very well together, which was fortunate as we had to keep him for three weeks before we could use him. His film career, as it turned out, was not very long.

The day of his big scene arrived and he was duly draped over a mopani branch framed in the foreground of the camera shot. Behind him the lions, followed by the intrepid Game Warden, walked nonchalantly across camera from left to right and out of the picture. They were not the only ones to leave. Charlie, conscious that his duties for the day were over and anxious to continue his siesta, simply continued up the mopani tree and disappeared into a convenient hole. It was the last time any of us saw him.

One day in the middle of filming our head producer from Salisbury arrived to see how the film was progressing. At the same time he had a special request to make. Could he direct a couple of shots, using Big Boy and Little Boy in character parts, for another film he was making? It concerned some of our early pioneers.

Apparently one of the first missionaries had been taken from his tent by a lion, and the producer wanted to recreate the scene. It called for two shots: one of a lion rushing into a tent, another of the lion rushing out. The rest of the film had already been shot.

This seemed simple enough and would no doubt have been so if the lions had been trained or disciplined. But they were not. Part of my object in bringing them up was to simulate their natural conditions as much as possible, and this did not include turning them into performing circus animals. They were therefore totally undisciplined. If they showed any tendency to turn on me I used to beat them off with the stick which I always carried with me. This is the sort of treatment they would have received from their mother and, as a result, we understood each other perfectly. I was the boss lion and there was no misunderstanding about our respective status. Any other situation would have been intolerable. But apart from this tacit agreement they could do what they wanted. They did, however, acknowledge a *food call*, which was useful if I wanted to call them up from the bush. But of course they only responded to it if they happened to be hungry.

I explained this to the producer, who appeared undeterred in his enthusiasm to go ahead. He had brought his own tent with him which he intended to use as a prop in the scene we were about to film. Would we put it up?

We did so. Under his instructions we also made up a camp-bed inside, with a dummy missionary lying asleep under the blanket. As the first shot was to be of a lion bounding through the entrance, we left the front flap open and cut a hole through the back of the tent through which the camera lens could unobtrusively protrude. To tempt the lion into the tent I would throw a piece of meat inside. To catch him again as he came out, we would simply move the camera and take another shot of him running out of the tent. Simple filming technique. Camera set. Sun in the correct position. Ready to roll.

But try as we did, Nelson and I could not get Big Boy on his own into the right position before the meat was thrown into the tent. As the lions were usually together it was sometimes difficult to separate them. Yet the shot called for only one lion to eat the missionary.

The producer was adamant about this. I wanted Big Boy for the shot, for I knew how temperamental and uncontrollable

Little Boy could be, but due to a misunderstanding Little Boy, who was nearer, rushed into the tent instead.

The camera clicked away merrily and the shot was a success. Now all we had to do was to change camera position to shoot the next sequence. But Little Boy had taken possession of the tent and nothing would induce him to move. He was like that when he took a fancy to something. And he liked the producer's tent. Even after he had finished the piece of meat he continued to growl and demonstrate and anyone who approached did so at the risk of being attacked. No one could get near the cameras.

After some thought, we decided to try and entice Little Boy away while we changed the camera position to the front of the tent. We would do the next shot with Big Boy coming out, and no one would know it was a different lion. After some coaxing with a nice juicy lump of buffalo meat, we managed to bribe Little Boy away from his lair. But the camera team were a little too hasty in going forward to move their equipment. From about fifty yards away, Little Boy suddenly lost interest in the meat Nelson was bribing him with and realised that certain people were trying to take over his precious tent. He charged back in swift, short bounds, with teeth bared, emitting that deep guttural grunt which is so peculiarly ominous and frightening.

The camera crew scattered. A thousand pounds-worth of Ariflex camera on its tripod crashed to the ground. Everywhere there was panic. Our itinerant film producer, in his haste to evacuate his ground, tripped over a tent rope and brought the tent down like a deflated parachute.

Bewildered, astonished to see his tent suddenly vanish before his eyes, Little Boy gave up his attack and returned to Nelson and the meat. He looked calm and bored.

To my shame I burst into uncontrollable laughter. The

producer, his face an ashen colour, strode back to camp without a word. Anker and Roger rather shamefacedly picked up their camera and started to collect their kit together. It was the end of filming for the day.

When we got back to camp our producer had already packed his bag. He instructed his team to pack up their equipment and leave for Salisbury the next morning; he was not prepared to allow his staff to be exposed to such danger. If he had known how uncontrollable the lions were going to be, he would never have agreed to the film being made in the first place.

I tried to explain that the shot we had just taken was not part of our script and that we were only obliging him by lending him the lions, but he was in no mood to listen to reason. I suppose it is not surprising. To be charged by a lion the first time you have ever seen one outside a zoo is enough to make even a film producer, who must have been exposed to all sorts of risks in the course of his career, somewhat indignant.

By morning, however, Anker and Roger had persuaded him to allow them to stay on and finish our film. Reluctantly he agreed, so long as they were prepared to risk it. But by the time we were set up for action he himself was many miles away on his return journey to Salisbury, out of reach of carnivorous film stars. A rather sadistic streak in me makes me wish I could have introduced him to Charlie.

In later years I was often asked whether I had seen my lions again and whether they recognised me. As I have explained, I did go back and look for Big Boy and Little Boy a year later and after some search found them in more or less the same area where I had abandoned them the previous season. They had joined up with a family of lions consisting of a big ginger-maned male, two lionesses and three fairly well-grown juveniles. When I came across them they were still feeding on a kill the pride had made the previous day. The carcass had been dragged into the shade of a spreading tamarind tree growing out of an ant-hill. Big Boy and Little Boy were feeding on the remnant of the buffalo while the rest of the pride, who had obviously had their fill, were sprawled about in the shadows in the manner of all lions who have just completed a banquet and are sleeping it off, indifferent to all that is going on around them.

This indifference, however, did not extend to allowing strangers to approach too close. They showed no signs of inquisitiveness up to about seventy yards, although they had been watching me all the time, but when I tried to get closer they shed their lethargy and sat up alert. As I came nearer still, one of the lionesses flattened her ears and began to flick her tail, an unmistakable warning in lion language. 'No further,' it said in capital letters.

Big Boy and Little Boy were on the far side of the group so I edged over to one side and called to them in a way I felt they would recognise, and which I had used to call them to food when they were younger. Both lions stopped eating when they heard the sound and stared at me. Big Boy walked towards me until he was about fifty yards away and then sat down staring straight into my eyes. Recognition was certainly there. Affection? Possibly, but it was not very clearly demonstrated. Little Boy did not even leave his meal.

I dared not approach closer because of the challenging growl from the lioness and in any case I had achieved what I came to do. I had found Big Boy and Little Boy. The fact that they were alive and healthy confirmed that all the trouble I had taken to prepare them for such a life was worth it. They were obviously successfully established in a wild state. If they could survive for a full year on their own it was a clear indication that they were perfectly capable of living out their full span in their new environment.

The fact that both lions were apparently indifferent to me was a blow to my parental pride. But it was one I had half-expected. Sentimentality is an unwarranted luxury in the wilds and I was no longer a member of their pride. Besides, Big Boy had not entirely forgotten me. The legend of Androcles and the lion makes a delightful Sunday school story and I am sure my book would have been all the richer had an affectionate and grateful Big Boy limped up to me to have a thorn extracted. But the facts compel me to curb my imagination.

My surmise is that Big Boy and Little Boy must have had a difficult time when they first took up domicile in this area. For the lions already established there would certainly have resented them as outsiders and no doubt roughed them up from time to time. On the other hand, as I had witnessed before I released them, they were quite capable of holding their own in a fight. If Big Boy and Little Boy had been normal wild lions seeking new territory they would have taken the hint after being attacked and would have moved on elsewhere. But in view of their rather unnatural upbringing they probably felt they had no alternative territory to move to. They would stay on sufferance, in spite of the challenge from the rightful estate owners, eventually hoping to become tolerated or accepted as part of the normal community provided they accepted a junior status.

Obviously, when I saw them, they were not accepted as full partners in the pride but were tolerated in the manner of camp followers. One day I imagine they would graduate to full status and be accepted into whatever place in the hierarchy they qualified for.

17. Concrete jungle

After *Return to the Wild* was published in 1962 and had some success, I was made rather a fuss of or, more appropriately, I was 'lionised', particularly in the Rhodesias where I was treated as the local boy who had made good.

I was human enough to be flattered by this praise, although at times being somewhat bewildered by it. What pleased me even more was that Nelson, who had played a major part in bringing up the lions, was also recognised. He lapped it up.

At that time the two Rhodesias and Nyasaland were part of the ill-fated Federation which has since broken up. But before it disbanded its Public Relations Department, taking advantage of our temporary fame, sent Nelson and me to London as part of their publicity campaign to introduce the people of the Federation to the everyday Englishman.

The purpose of our inclusion in their programme was two-fold: first, to bring the Federation's wildlife and tourist potential to the notice of the public and secondly, to emphasise the 'partnership' aspect of the Federation, where the white man and African could work together in harmony.

To Nelson, who had spent his whole life in the bush, the revelations of the civilised world were shattering. We are so used to the achievements of modern science that we take them completely for granted. It is difficult for us to see them as if for the first time through the eyes of an unsophisticated man. Even so, it should not be difficult to imagine Nelson's astonishment at his first introduction to the inside of an aeroplane.

As we were travelling to London as V.I.P.s, the Captain of the Comet IV invited us both, once we had reached cruising height, into the cockpit. The array of clocks, dials and instruments was dazzling and Nelson watched them with thrilled fascination. They were, of course, beyond his comprehension, but when the Skipper pointed out our course on a map, Nelson understood its purpose. He had watched me making maps in the Luangwa Valley.

Delighted by his interest, I went on to try and explain the principles of radar as we began to descend over London through a thick blanket of fog. I should have known better. For the language that Nelson speaks has a very limited vocabulary. It is mostly confined to the fundamental necessities of village life; even common domestic commodities like a box or a table, which were unknown before the advent of the European, have no name in his language; his tribe merely use the white man's word for them and add an appropriate vowel on the end. But I could not resist it. In the middle of my exposition on the use of electronics in guiding aircraft on to an invisible runway, I was disappointed to see that Nelson was not particularly impressed. He was looking at me rather quizzically, as if I were being stupid. His expression was familiar to me. I had seen the same look on his face when we were hunting together, trying to unravel a particularly difficult spoor. If I were leading and had taken up a stale track, he would let me go on for some time before pointing out with just this expression that I was doing very well but that the trail we were following was at least twenty-four hours old. I recognised it now and asked him why he didn't believe me. He hastened to explain that he believed me all right, but he could not understand why it was so difficult; after all, the pilot had a map – all he had to do was follow it.

This attitude, of course, makes life much easier – why clutter our brains with things we cannot understand! A simple being enjoys so much more pleasure than a complicated 'mixed-up' one; and anything unaccountable can be written off as white man's medicine. Consequently the wonders of London which impressed Nelson most were the simple things which could be easily demonstrated. Even I was infected by his enthusiasm when we first encountered a self-opening glass door operated by some photo-electric device. Nelson's amazement when the door opened of its own accord was well worth seeing. He insisted on us going through the door several times, his expression of astonishment increasing each time. Then, with an air of nonchalance, as if trying to deceive a wounded animal, he walked parallel to the door without displaying his intention and when he got opposite it made a sudden dash sideways so as to take it unawares. The door opened. Nelson walked through shaking his head in bewilderment, oblivious of the small crowd which had gathered to watch this uninhibited performance.

Although we went about together I was rather worried that during our wanderings in London Nelson and I might become separated. As his knowledge of the English language was limited to a few words of greeting, I could imagine his feeling of loneliness and fear if he should become lost in this seething mass of humanity. One of our first calls on the day after we landed was to a large departmental store in Oxford Street where I bought him a suit. He was thrilled and extremely proud of it. Years later, whenever he went back to his village he would unpack his suit on special occasions and, from the elevated status of one who has been to London, he would recount some of the wonders of the white man's world. But while still there I had written his address on a card to which I had pinned a pound note. This he kept in his breast pocket, together with instructions in English to get a taxi to take him straight to his lodgings if we should ever become separated.

I need not have worried. He stuck to my side as closely as a pilot fish to a shark, even in the underground when we were packed in like sardines in a tin and even during the rush-hour when the pavements were swarming with a hurrying mass of people struggling and scrumming to escape from their eight-hour prison sentence.

At first I tried to get Nelson to walk by my side so that I could keep an eye on him, but he was determined to walk behind. In spite of our common role in London and the fact that we ate together and lived in the same hotel, it was impossible to break down the master-servant relationship. To walk alongside me would be a display of familiarity and discourtesy which he was not prepared to give.

It is the moments of turmoil and congestion that will remain in Nelson's memory far more vividly than the white man's steel and concrete wonders which were pointed out to him with such pride. Because of the contrast to his familiar peaceful, unhurried existence in Africa he will remember the jostling crowds and the inordinately hurried tempo of life. Only in the termite mounds, or when the locusts invade his land, does he ever see anything to approach the hysterical mass-activity of a modern city: the bewilderment, if he could so phrase it, of a concrete jungle.

18. The white princess

After experiencing the delights of an English spring I returned to the Luangwa Valley to find all the migrant birds had departed, some to their chosen breeding grounds within the continent of Africa, many to Europe and Asia and some even to the Arctic circle. Always they are drawn northwards as by some invisible magnet, never to the south. It is as if a mysterious clarion call had sounded, heralding the awakening spring to the north.

What tells them the days are lengthening in those far lands where on arrival they will enjoy fifteen or more hours of daylight to hawk for insects and feed their voracious young? The European swallows, some of our last emigrants to leave, had already departed, carrying with them our good wishes. Many of them would not live through the perilous hazards of their journey; the weak would be eliminated but the species would survive. We were now left, sadly diminished, with our permanent boarders and the approach of the cold season.

In June it can be chilly at dawn before the sun rises sufficiently to disperse the early morning mist. It can also be very beautiful. The scene I watched on one occasion was more than that: it was also exciting, with that strange thrilling sense of discovering something new and unknown.

I had taken up a position in a glade of magnificent winter thorns, where I was eavesdropping on fairyland. The outlines of the giant clean-limbed trees were shimmering and ghostly in the haze. At the far end of the stage the mist was gently rising from the dark mirror surface of the lagoon.

I watched spellbound and fascinated as she picked her way delicately through the mist, occasionally stopping to lift her head to inhale the scent-laden morning air, seemingly disdainful of the drab, commonplace sisters who were escorting her to the pool. Pure white she was.

My mind was immediately transported back to my childhood, to the time when my mother used to read us bedtime stories, and I remembered the beautiful, enchanting illustration of Snow White. I called this apparition the Princess and have conceded her royal status ever since, for the divine right of kings and queens was never more eloquently demonstrated. She is probably the only pure white impala the world has ever known.

Albino can be a derogatory word and I cannot have my Princess associated with the term. In any case albinos have pink eyes which quiver in the bright light, but my Princess has eyes which are perfectly normal and therefore she cannot be a true albino. Besides which, I prefer my own fairy-book image.

Albinism, of course, occurs in different degrees. I have seen several cases of this mutation among other wild animals. For many years in the late 1940s there lived a white kudu which was often seen along the Lutembwe River, twenty-odd miles from Fort Jameson. As always with these quirks of nature, local superstition credited the animal with all kinds of supernatural powers and, although this kudu lived in an area which was heavily hunted, it survived its full span of a dozen years without the slightest risk of falling to a hunter's rifle. Then there was the white buffalo which was shot on the Northern Rhodesia-Tanganyika border during the rinderpest campaign in the early years of the war. Currently there exists a well-known white giraffe in the Rukwa area in the southern parts of Tanganyika (now Tanzania). Many other examples occur from time to time but I have never seen an animal so perfectly white as my Princess, nor one quite so beautiful. One wonders to what extent this would affect her chance of survival against predators. But since animals are colour-blind, to a lion or leopard she would probably appear only slightly paler than other impala.

I have followed closely the welfare of the White Princess, whose territory lies within a few miles of my camp in the Luangwa Valley Game Reserve. Her existence as a faun was first rumoured late in 1960 but it was not until the following year that I was able to confirm the truth of this report. Since then the herd of which she is a member has created a good deal of interest and its movement has been regularly observed and recorded.

Knowledge of the movements of animals is a most important factor in the management of a sanctuary and some ingenious techniques have been devised for marking animals in order to keep them under observation. You must be able to identify the animal or group you are studying very positively, so that its movement can be plotted on a map and its range thereby determined. In the case of this particular impala, nature has provided all the identification marks necessary. Never could an animal be more conspicuous. It is hardly surprising, therefore, that its range has been fairly accurately recorded.

Like all other wild creatures, impala have a fairly well defined range, which would of course vary in extent according to the nature of the habitat. In typical scrub bush or woodland the range of each group is limited to a comparatively small area. The area covered by the white impala's herd, which I have plotted on a map, is one and a half miles in length and only half a mile across. There is usually some overlapping with neighbouring herds but normally, when conditions are favourable, the impala live and die within these limits. This *home range* where they obtain food, water, shelter, and everything else they need for their survival is quite different from their *territory*, which is defended and is usually only a small part of the home range.

These terms, which are often confused by amateur naturalists, warrant some comment. The instinct to possess and defend a territory is universal throughout the animal kingdom. It is one of the fundamental laws of nature originating many millions of years ago, although our knowledge of the subject is relatively new. It was only in the 1920s that Eliot Howard, a well-known English ornithologist, first presented the world with his findings in his book, *Territory in Birdlife*. And it was not until many years afterwards that it was realised that this practice was also common to mammals and played a very vital part in the perpetuation of the species.

It is said that the urge to acquire territory is even stronger than the sex urge, that combat between two animals is not directly for sexual victory but for territory or, in the case of social animals, for status. Only after these preliminary combats, where superiority is established and territory or status acquired, will mating take place.

Eliot Howard also points out that it is very rare for a bird to mate which has not first of all established a territory and, moreover, that a bird which has staked out its territory hardly ever fails to find a female. A great number of those which fail to win space for themselves are relegated to a season of unrewarded bachelorhood.

The beautiful bird-songs which are such a delight to hear on a spring morning are not, as we romantically believe, an expression of joy and happiness. The heuglins robin bursting forth in melodious song from his perch on a nearby acacia is, we are told, declaring belligerently to all the rest of his species to lay off – or else!

These principles apply with equal force to all animals. In the case of a gregarious species, such as the impala, there is a very strict hierarchy involved: that is to say, an order of precedence in which Number One dominates Number Two and Number Two dominates Number Three and so on down the scale to the unfortunate Last in Line who gets pushed around by everybody. This is commonly referred to as a *pecking order* and is only established as a result of combat, sometimes by serious fighting but more often by mutual consent when a less aggressive animal accepts dominance by another, without apparently contesting the issue. These basic principles of behaviour apply equally to impala. But, apart from this generalisation, very little is really known about the specific social organisation of impala. This is doubly surprising since this animal is the commonest antelope in Africa. Yet I have never met or heard of anyone who has seen an impala mating.

When I first saw my Princess she was a member of a group of twenty to twenty-five ewes. All status combat had already taken place and the herd was ruled by a fine upstanding ram in the prime of life. Several other bachelor groups occupied the same home range, but as this was not rutting time the other rams did not seem to want to dispute his authority. This was not a permanent distribution, because the composition of a herd varies considerably throughout the season. But, on the whole it seems to be regulated principally by the territorial-status conflict and by the breeding cycle of the ewes.

During the early months of the year when the country is

subject to heavy rain there is no very strict segregation of the sexes. Some time later the males gather together and begin their rutting behaviour, which continues for several weeks. The deep hollow-sounding bark of the rams is taken up by one after another as they chase each other in circles, cavorting and prancing in bursts of exuberance until the whole territory resounds to the noise of their chorus. As they prance, stiff-legged, they erect their tails which flash conspicuously like raised white flags inviting any male in the vicinity to join in the charade. At this stage there is no serious fighting; this comes later when some order of dominance has been created. Then the combat is far more aggressive and deliberate, and it is significant that it is performed with little noise other than the sickening thud of the horns crashing together. At this stage, combat often results in serious injuries.

During these rutting demonstrations there does not appear to be any clear-cut division between the various groups, although the ewes, with last season's lambs, keep together and the youngsters are sometimes seen huddling in nursery groups. No hierarchy or pecking order has yet been established for the coming season, and these preliminary bouts continue for many weeks until finally all the weaker contenders are eliminated and the victor earns his reward: the right to dominate and cover the ewes in his domain. These ewes now become his property and he jealously guards them against the amorous advances of the young bucks. The right of the champion to monopolise a dozen or more delectable maidens, while his male companions live an existence of enforced celibacy, is rarely disputed. When such a challenge is presented the champion will defend his title belligerently, and with traditional right on his side to give him added confidence he is rarely deposed.

Ultimately the herds are established in groups of a dozen or more females with their dominant ram, while the less fortunate rams make up smaller bachelor parties. The young bucks of last season's crop herd together in their own teenager groups and stand out conspicuously with their short, straight horns which have not yet started to curve. Towards the end of April the females are sired. The gestation period lasts about 180 days, after which, in the last days of October, they begin to drop their fawns. At this time, with his biological purpose fulfilled, the proprietary interest of the herd ram diminishes.

A few days before the young is expected, the gravid ewe breaks away from her group, retiring to some discreet covert where she can produce her fawn in reasonable seclusion. The fawn remains hidden in the grass or thicket during the first few days of its life while the mother browses in the vicinity, every now and again returning to suckle her offspring. When she feels her baby is competent enough to take its place among the more vigorous members of the herd, they both return. By this time several other mothers and fawns have appeared.

It is one of the most fascinating and beautiful scenes imaginable to see these playful, leggy creatures, exact replicas of their mothers, gambolling and bouncing about and chasing shadows just for the sheer joy of living. Their mothers go unconcernedly about their normal business until one of the youngsters requires nourishment and seeks his mother. How he distinguishes her is a mystery to me for they all look exactly alike. When he finds her his little head butts her underbelly vigorously until he has secured a good hold of her udder and can satisfy his hunger.

There was an exciting atmosphere of expectancy and conjecture among the few of us who lived in the game reserve at the end of October 1962. Our very special White Impala was two years old and expecting her first fawn. Would it be normal or would it be pure white like its mother? Never had an event in the game reserve been anticipated with such interest. The more romantic among us were convinced we would be blessed with a lovely baby as snow white as its mother. But the more prosaic members of our little community, who had made a study of the genetical factors involved, were sceptical and informed us that the chances were less than one in a million.

They were right of course. Her baby was a perfectly ordinary brown fawn. So were its successors. For, as I write, the White Princess is seven years old, which is well past middle age for an impala, and the mother of many fawns.

Long may she continue to reign: supreme in her beauty, unique in her appearance, whatever the colour of her young.

CONSERVATIONIST

19. The overcrowded ark

When I returned to the Luangwa Valley to investigate its wild life and to put forward some suggestions for its management, I found the assignment a pretty tall order, for the area included several game reserves, as well as the vast marginal areas which support few people but a great many wild animals. The human and animal populations outside the game reserves are an integral part of the ecology and I had to show that their interests did not necessarily conflict, that it was possible for both communities to live together in harmony.

Due to seasonal floods, lack of communications and the presence of tsetse fly, normal farming development was out of the question. The best use that could be made of this land was to turn its wildlife resources into cash revenue, to make wild animals pay. Only if I could put forward a plan which would show some financial reward would it prove acceptable. It was easy enough to know the solution but quite another thing to persuade the authorities to agree. Any proposition for instance which restricted the privileges of the local tribesmen in any way was virtually doomed from the start.

At that time, under Colonial rule, the interests of the inhabitants in the tribal areas were paramount, and this was interpreted by some to mean that no measure of control could be introduced, however beneficial, if it were unpopular with the tribes themselves.

It was also apparent that no long term solution for the future of wildlife could be found without tying in all aspects of conservation – agriculture, forestry, veterinary – as well as the complex requirements of the human inhabitants. Ideally, to do this well a comprehensive land-usage survey would have had to be carried out by a team of experts. But funds were short and to obtain the services of personnel qualified to take on such a task was then virtually impossible.

By way of compromise I co-opted several field officers from departments which had an interest in the Luangwa Valley, and it was through this committee that I operated. A report was finally submitted to the Government, filed away and forgotten: 1960 was not a good year to introduce controversial ideas; the Government was too embarrassed trying to reconcile the impatient demands for Nationalism to bother very much about less urgent matters.

We did, however, sow a seed which fortunately was to germinate later when the new African Government came into power. During my survey I had become greatly concerned with the problem of over stocking in the game reserve, with its consequent dangers of deterioration. Among other recommendations in our report, therefore, we proposed a limited 'cropping' scheme, aimed at reducing the surplus stock and simultaneously earning some money for the local treasury from the sale of meat. Although the report was relegated to the dusty archives of the Secretariat, the cropping idea stayed in circulation, to be trundled out by successive game wardens when anyone with influence was willing to lend a sympathetic ear.

Eventually the project received the blessing of the Food and

Agricultural Organisation of the United Nations, and an operation far more comprehensive than the modest one we envisaged has since materialised. A large modern abattoir and cold storage plant has been erected near the game reserve, designed to handle all the meat from the surplus animals which have to be culled.

The Game Department deserves considerable credit for pioneering such an ambitious cropping scheme, the nature and magnitude of which has never before been known in Africa. The object is to reduce the surplus animal population and to restore a balance commensurate with the carrying-capacity of the land. At the moment experts are carrying out a detailed research programme to determine this factor accurately. All the major types of vegetation have been mapped out and experiments are being undertaken to test the effects of fire, grazing, and the fencing-off of sample areas. The diet of the main herbivores is being investigated and the biology of the food plants studied.

At the same time other biologists are studying the number, population structure, movements and diseases of elephant, hippo and buffalo, which are the only animals to be cropped in the scheme's initial stages. This is a vast programme and could only be carried through by a team of men trained in different disciplines: the field naturalist with his notebook and binoculars, carefully studying animals in the field; the botanist with his hand-lens and collecting press; the biologist counting buffalo from a low-flying aeroplane or painting identification numbers on an elephant anaesthetised by a dart gun, for studying its subsequent movements; the veterinary scientist with his microscope; the cropping ranger with his lethal dart gun.

It may take a long time before this survey is completed and

all the data correctly interpreted, but meanwhile a start has been made to reduce some of the surplus population. The initial target in the first year has been set at five hundred elephant, the same number of hippo, and a thousand buffalo. When one realises that a large elephant weighs between six or seven tons, a hippo more than two tons, and a buffalo a ton and a half, the extent of this operation in terms of meat alone can easily be imagined. The rate of culling is of course liable to be increased or decreased as experience dictates, but once a balance has been achieved a regular annual crop can be harvested. In a healthy community, this could amount to between five and ten per cent of the animal population.

In most preserves in Europe and America a much bigger percentage (from 25 to 50 per cent) is taken off every year to keep the numbers stable. Admittedly, these continents rarely have a predator factor to contend with, so the problems are not completely parallel. But the success of these countries, where culling techniques are so highly developed, does give us a good idea of the large crop that can be harvested from a well-managed range.

America, for instance, gained many years on Britain in her modern approach to, and management of, wildlife sanctuaries. It seems rather sad that in the days when Britain had an empire and was responsible for most of the best wildlife sanctuaries in the world, there were so few facilities for the practical training of her young men in the techniques of wildlife management. Of course she lacked the impetus of having national parks and game reserves of her own, but none of her universities made special instruction available in this field. Today nearly every university in America offers a course in some aspect of ecology, wildlife or range management. Enthusiastic young men trained in these sciences are drafted to the national parks or game reserves throughout the States. Some also find their way to Africa.

The cropping scheme in the Luangwa Valley has caused a great deal of interest – and controversy – among various international organisations, and some of the world's most eminent ecologists have visited the Valley to make their reports. Without exception they confirm the need for cropping and give their blessing to what is now being done to correct the chronic ill-effects resulting from over-population.

The end product of overcrowding is obvious to those on the spot, but is not always so clear to the layman. As the numbers of animals increase and more of the available food is used up, the animals begin to lose condition badly as less food has to fill more bellies. This lack of condition is shown first of all at the base of the tail; instead of a sleek fat rump the root of the tail, which acts as a fatty reservoir in healthy animals, becomes angular and droops. Then, as deterioration continues, the pelvic bones become visible and in the more advanced stage the ribs begin to show. Animals are now very vulnerable to diseases which they normally resist. They are open, too, to epidemics and if they succumb a crash in population results that can be catastrophic and may even lead to wholesale disease and mortality.

One of the manifestations of over-population happens when the land loses its top-soil; the roots of the perennial grasses will become exposed and, instead of covering the whole surface evenly, will tend to form clumps with the roots elevated on pedestals several inches above the ground. The rain water then runs off, forming gullies, and progressive erosion sets in.

Once the habitat is ruined by over-population and erosion takes place, nature needs ten thousand years to replace one inch of soil, whereas with intelligent control the population of a well-managed sanctuary can be doubled within ten years. Perhaps this illustration will help to emphasise a point I stressed earlier: that it is much more important to conserve the habitat than to protect the animals.

The danger signals are obvious to the well-trained field man, and so are the implications. But they are not always so apparent to the uninitiated. It does not need an expert to see the destruction caused by elephants in places where the devastation is quite spectacular, where acre upon acre of trees have been flattened to resemble a battlefield after an artillery barrage. But it does need a more critical eye to evaluate the exact effect of this so-called damage. Some trees and vegetation provide more valuable fodder than others, and only when a trend of progressive deterioration threatens the more valuable plant species is it possible to see and assess the overall effect on the habitat.

For instance, when you travel through any well-populated elephant area in the Luangwa Valley you will notice large areas of copsed-down mopani bushes. They are not, as you may at first think, young trees or bushes; they are fully mature, stunted trees that have been kept down to bush size by browsing elephants. This copsing, if not done to excess, can be beneficial. The mopani is the predominant tree in the Valley and in its perfect state is a tall clean-limbed tree as large as an elm, but quite inaccessible to browsing animals. But, as a bush, it comes within reach of the impala and other smaller browsing animals, which consume it avidly. This food would not be available to them if it were not kept down to bush-like size by elephants. Who is to say, then, whether this constitutes damage?

A certain amount of tree felling, too, is a normal process in any elephant country and is part of the valuable conversion cycle which should be continually taking place in a well-adjusted biotic community. No organic matter is really

Compare this mopani woodland that has been destroyed by excessive elephant population with the fine stand of mopani on the next page. Below, hippo are responsible for far more damage to the riverine habitat than the elephant

Baobab tree eaten by elephants; 'Tirelessly they tease away at the soft fibrous tree with their tusks and pull off the loosened fibres with their trunks . . . when the whole thing is undermined it collapses'

wasted. The uprooted tree exposes the ground, which is aerated; the broken-down tree rots; micro-organisms are formed which return to the soil and fertilise further vegetation to feed more animals; and so the nitrogen cycle continues. What to an untrained eye may look like damage might be actually beneficial. It is only when the processes are accelerated by *over*-usage that danger becomes imminent, and it is up to the trained field man rather than the visiting specialist to discern these signs before conditions become critical. Specialists exist for emergencies and to suggest remedial measures.

Oddly enough, elephants' feeding habits serve a useful purpose in the way of seed dispersal; many of the trees they break down are attacked seasonally only for the fruit they bear. The seeds of the fruit are passed out in the droppings and in this way new trees are planted far and wide during the elephants' wanderings. Elephants are particularly fond of the fruit from the marula tree (*Sclerocarya*), which bears prolifically from May onwards. In a wide circle around the base of every marula tree the ground is trampled flat by elephants, which hang around for days feeding on the round crab-apple-like fruit. Every now and then one will lay its trunk perpendicularly against the massive tree and push with its head and body in a colossal lunging motion, shaking the tree and causing the marulas to rain to the ground. Then, together with its companions, it will pick up the fruit one at a time with the finger-like process at the end of the trunk and transfer it to its mouth. This unhurried process goes on for hours each day until the tree has shed its last fruit. Then the elephants move on to another tree.

These are the fruit which according to popular belief make elephants drunk and cause them to behave in an extraordinary fashion. The fruit is supposed to ferment in the elephant's stomach and make the animal drunk. But although it needs no great imagination to visualise a group of roistering elephants staggering home from a marula party, I think the proper place for such thoughts is the comic strip. I have never believed this oft-repeated fable or received any evidence in its support, and am rather surprised that so many people who ought to know better should continue to believe it.

Another valuable fodder tree, the winter thorn (*Acacia albida*), is also greatly sought after. Elephants move in from far and wide to the alluvium glades where these magnificent trees grow in order to enjoy the seed pods when they ripen in September. These pods, which resemble dried apple rings, are highly nutritious. Chemical analysis has shown that they contain as much as 50 per cent carbohydrate and over 10 per cent protein.

The pods are shaken down by the elephants and become easily available to the impala and other animals, who could not otherwise reach them. It is fascinating to watch a group of elephants feeding from these trees on the banks of a lagoon. If the tree is too massive to shake, an elephant will stretch up its trunk and tear down one of the lower branches to get at the pods; in well-used elephant country very few of these lower limbs remain, so it has to stand on its back legs, lifting its fore-feet and extending its trunk perpendicularly to reach up to a phenomenal height – for all the world like a performing elephant in a circus – in order to reach the nearest branch. I have actually measured the reach of an elephant stretching up in this way. It extended for more than twenty-four feet.

When a small bachelor party is feeding and the boss bull shakes some pods down for himself, he strongly resents sharing the proceeds with any of the others. Sometimes a young bull, lacking the strength to shake one of these giant trees, tries to sneak a few tasty morsels, but Big Brother has other ideas and with spreading ears and flashing tusks he rushes at the impudent young bull, who runs away squealing cravenly. Not that this admonition seems to deter him for long. He comes back again and again, deliberately to torment Big Brother. There is never a dull moment watching elephants on these occasions.

Unfortunately the good work an elephant contributes in propagating this tree is nullified by the damage he simultaneously inflicts. During the long periods spent in the vicinity of these winter thorns elephants like to vary their diet by feeding on the bark. Consequently many trees are completely ring-barked. This magnificent tree, to my mind the most beautiful in the riverine zone and probably the most valuable fodder tree in the Valley, is therefore being gradually eliminated. Even though the seeds distributed in the droppings germinate freely and the struggling young seedlings make a brave effort to establish themselves, the competition is too great and they never survive for long before they are eaten back again by the lesser grazing animals. For many years now I have not seen one single young winter thorn which has established itself beyond the seedling stage. It is a matter for great regret.

A more unusual phenomenon which is apparent to anyone who is familiar with the feeding habits of elephants in this area is their newly acquired taste for the baobab tree. When I first came to the Luangwa Valley I never saw a single baobab eaten by elephants. And yet today it has become one of their favourite foods and towards the end of the dry season hardly a tree remains that has not been eaten into. Tirelessly they tease away at the soft fibrous tree with their tusks and pull off the loosened fibres with their trunks, returning day after day to the same tree until they have excavated a huge cavity in the massive trunk. When the whole thing is undermined it collapses, but they still continue to eat away voraciously after the giant has fallen.

The baobab has a colossal girth; a dozen men surrounding the tree with outstretched arms, finger-tip to finger-tip, would barely encompass a medium-sized specimen. This tree has an entirely different texture from any other I know. In most trees the sap, their life blood, is carried through the inner skin underlying the bark (known as the phloem) and when it is ring-barked, as so often happens, the tree gets no further nourishment and dies. But this is not the case with the baobab; even when the surface has been deeply eaten into around the whole circumference the tree continues to live until it collapses.

Baobabs grow to a very old age and carbon tests (the technique known as C14 which has been developed to determine the antiquity of fossils) have shown that some of the larger trees now standing were in existence many years before the birth of Christ. It would be a sad loss if these fantastic landmarks, so typical of our low-lying valleys, were to be lost to us through bad range management.

Leaving the sentimental view on one side, there must be a sound biological reason why elephants have within the last dozen years so changed their feeding habits that they are now eliminating the baobab trees. The tree is known to have a very high calcium content and it may be that with the increase in elephant numbers in recent years other sources of this mineral have been depleted and the animals have had to adapt their feeding habits to make up for the deficiency.

I know of at least another dozen species of trees and plants whose depletion can be directly attributed to over-population in the game reserves of the Luangwa Valley. And these are just a few of the more obvious manifestations of imbalance.

Although I have written about elephants as the most spectacular offenders other animals, too, are causing similar, although perhaps less conspicuous, damage. Hippo are by far the worst culprits. Due to their mode of life and their very restricted range, their feeding is confined to the immediate riverine zone. Unlike an elephant, which has a wide choice of food, a hippo is purely a grazer and lives exclusively on grass. Because of this selective feeding in a concentrated area the damage to the soil cover is proportionately far greater than if the feeding were more varied and spread over a wider territory, particularly when hippo occur in large numbers.

Due to their extensive movement it is difficult to assess the number of elephants in the Luangwa Valley but over the last two years a constant study of their movements and population has been undertaken from the air and on the ground. These surveys have been made during successive seasons and have produced a fairly accurate census totalling 23,000 elephant distributed over approximately 12,000 square miles, a density of about two per square mile. The distribution of hippo on the other hand is far more concentrated. The last hippo count along the game reserve frontage showed a total of 8,000 in just over 100 miles of river. Assuming that a hippo's feeding range is normally not more than a mile and a half on either side of the river, this shows a density of more than ten times that of the elephant. When you consider that each hippo consumes several hundred pounds of grass every day, you can imagine the enormous quantity of food taken by this animal alone, in addition to the thousands of other animals which concentrate along the river.

It is this evidence that spells disaster. Something positive must be done to allay the destructive process taking place. True, nature has her own ways of adjusting the balance, but her methods can sometimes be both drastic and prolonged; for she reckons time not in years but in centuries. A striking example of her methods occurred at the close of the last century. Towards the end of the 1890s, the wild animal population cycle in Africa seemed to reach a peak. Habitats became degraded, animals lost condition and their natural resistance was reduced so that they became infected with disease. The rinderpest epidemic, which started in East Africa, swept southward down the continent leaving millions of dead animals in its wake; vast populations were reduced to a few pitiful survivors. The epidemic finished in South Africa, where it decimated herds of cattle and sheep.

It has taken more than sixty years for the wild animals to build up again. Should we, then, let nature do her worst and take a chance on our great-great-grandchildren being able to enjoy the pleasure of our game reserve? Or should we give nature a helping hand so that we, and our sons and daughters, may benefit from such foresight?

In the past it was believed that the only purpose of a national park was to preserve its inhabitants, to allow them to multiply in peace, and to provide facilities for the public to visit them at will: in other words, to provide a refuge where the animals could live and breed secure against human predators. The idea was to leave it to nature.

This attitude served its purpose during that critical period when Africa was being opened up and wildlife was in danger of being exterminated by indiscriminate slaughter. The sanctuaries offered a valuable temporary respite at a time when little was known about game management, but this concept of a sanctuary is no longer tenable in the light of present knowledge. Habitat is the key to any wildlife sanctuary and protection is no substitute for it.

20. Wildlife management

Habitat is never constant. For various reasons biotic communities are always in some process of change. I have seen vegetation in certain parts of the Luangwa Valley change completely within half a man's lifetime; I have seen large areas of scrub-bush encroach where at one time there were open glades with scattered trees; I have seen extensive stretches of yellow thorn (*Acacia kirkii*) completely eliminated in an even shorter period, changing a well wooded area into an open scrub plain.

Two American ecologists, who are at the moment working on an ecological survey in the Luangwa Valley under the auspices of the Food and Agricultural Organisation, have uncovered some aerial photographs made in the 1930s. They have compared these with recent photographs. The change in thirty-five years is frightening, for with a change in habitat comes a corresponding change in the animal community it supports.

Many changes in habitat are caused by natural means, that is to say they are the result of physical laws rather than of man's activities. Thus a river may cut a new channel for itself making one area wetter, another drier. This is how the lagoons and oxbows of the riverine area are formed.

In the Luangwa Game Reserve there is a large grass plain, about ten square miles in extent, known as Lion Plain. When I first visited this place it was mopani woodland; in 1959 the Luangwa River cut another channel, slightly upstream from where the plain now is. As a result, this area of mopani woodland was 'drowned' and a grass plain formed. This is an example of a natural change in habitat. Such changes are very common in riverine areas where the vegetation is determined by the drainage.

Man, too, can influence, can indeed drastically alter, these natural processes. If he does not properly control the catchment areas of streams and rivers, for instance, most of the rainfall will run directly over the ground and into the river. This leads to dramatic 'flash floods' which gouge river banks at a spectacular rate. He can also alter, or control, by fire.

Bush fires are a very common feature of the African scene in the dry season. In fact they are so common that a layman could be excused for thinking that all the ordinary trees of miombo woodland must be immune to fire, else how are they still there? Surprisingly enough this is not the case, and the ubiquitous Brachystegia, Isoberlinia and Julbernadia species (collectively referred to sometimes as 'miombo') can all be destroyed by fire. This has been proved by Trapnell, who was a government ecologist in Northern Rhodesia before the war and who wrote a classical study of the vegetation, soils and agricultural system of the country. I met him on several occasions when I was employed on elephant control, but in those days I was regrettably only keen on hunting and was not interested enough to try and absorb anything he might be able to teach me from his vast knowledge of the country.

Trapnell's experiments proved that annual burning in October destroys the miombo woodland and results in open grassland. But if the wood is burnt in May, the woodland becomes thicker, the grasses correspondingly less dense. This is because the trees burn more fiercely in October, when the whole countryside is parched, than in May when there is still a mantle of greenness from the previous rainy season. Strangely enough it is in October, during the driest time of the year, that the sap rises and the miombo trees produce their new leaves and are therefore more vulnerable to destruction by fire.

There is another way in which man can alter the natural habitat – by controlling the grazing pressure. In some cases this has an immediate and direct effect, as when grazing destroys a particular plant species or results in the increase of some unpalatable species; for instance, when *hyparrhenia* grassland is heavily grazed there is a corresponding increase in the unpalatable spear grass, *Heteropogon contortus*.

In other cases, though, heavy grazing may have the opposite effect and actually increase the value of an area. The Luangwa Valley itself provides an example of this. In the riverine area there are large expanses of the tall unpalatable *Rottboellia*, yet within these one commonly finds 'grazing lawns' of more palatable grasses. These lawns are established on animal droppings and heavy grazing where trampling encourages the prostrate grasses.

Grazing, however, achieves its most spectacular effect when it is combined with burning. In the cattle ranching areas of South Africa there are large areas of open grassland which have been changed into woodland within the last few years by over-grazing. Ranchers speak of this process as 'bush encroachment'. These areas were originally treeless because the soil was fertile enough to support a dense cover of grass. Now the trees which grow naturally on these soils are species of *Acacia*, *Combretum* and *Afromosia*, all of which can be destroyed by fire. Before the advent of civilised man periodical sweeping fires every few years were a natural process and kept the trees back. If the intensity of fire is decreased, as it will if cattle graze off most of the top cover, then the trees will colonise. As soon as the trees grow they will compete with the grass, and the grass cover will get less and less as the trees increase. Hence bush encroachment is a self-perpetuating process which can only be stopped if the rancher both kills the trees by burning them and at the same time reduces the grazing pressure.

As well as altering the type of vegetation, fire and grazing can also affect the extent of soil erosion. The general principle here is that there should be a good vegetation cover at the start of the rains; if rain falls on bare ground, then erosion takes place and in hilly areas spectacular gullies will form.

You can see then how, in theory at least, any habitat can be tailored to suit any requirement. But who is to decide what these requirements are and what is to be done about them? Do you want scrub bush and thicket, which favour browsing animals, or open savannah for the grazers?

These problems, of course, can only be resolved if the authority responsible for the management of the sanctuary has a clear cut policy. The original concept of *protection* is not far-reaching enough to identify this purpose. Its aims must be more clearly defined. What is to be its goal?

I do not think anyone would argue if this should be to maintain or recreate conditions that prevailed at some earlier stage before man-made conditions began to affect the natural state of the sanctuary. But this cannot be done merely by sitting back and 'protecting' the area. It will need endless care and manipulation. To achieve this successfully, the *purpose* of each sanctuary must first be clearly defined, and the management pattern planned accordingly.

In July 1962 the First World Conference on National Parks was convened in Seattle and the recommendations resulting from these discussions were most enlightening. They established in unequivocal terms the modern concept of 'managing' rather than 'protecting' wildlife sanctuaries.

Few of the world's parks, as was pointed out, are large enough to be self-regulatory ecological units; they are, rather, ecological islands subject to direct or indirect modification by activities and conditions in surrounding areas. The point was emphasised that biotic communities are in a constant state of change and that in these 'successional' communities it is necessary to manage the habitat to achieve or stabilise it at a desired stage.

The Conference also made the point that where animal populations get out of balance with their habitat and threaten the continued existence of a desired environment population control becomes essential. This may become necessary in situations where ungulate populations have exceeded the carrying capacity of their habitat through loss of predators, immigration from surrounding areas, or compression of normal migratory population.

This question of the restriction of migrational pattern applies particularly to elephants in the Luangwa Valley, where in the past elephants wandered freely across Northern Rhodesia between the Congo border and Nyasaland. When I first visited the Valley there existed well-worn elephant roads between these borders. Elephants have a flair for choosing the best gradients in hilly country, and these routes were used by early travellers as bush paths; later these became tracks and eventually graduated to motor roads. Many highways existing today were once old elephant roads, although nowadays most of these migration roads have been restricted by human settlement and being no longer used, have become overgrown.

These are some of the reasons why the Game Department in

Zambia has recently embarked on a cropping scheme in the Luangwa Valley, yet there are still many people who believe implicitly in the sublime power of nature to heal her own ills and who contend that every animal in a game reserve should be sacrosanct. Fortunately, the modern concept of conservation is becoming more generally proven. Enlightened people accept the fact that nature might need a helping hand to adjust her mistakes. But this knowledge still does not prevent thousands of animal lovers and societies from all over the world deliberately blinding themselves to the true facts and spearheading campaigns to try and have what they call 'needless slaughter' stopped.

One should be thankful, therefore, that the authorities are sufficiently strong-minded and sensible to pursue their own course, and that they have had the courage to override public opinion which has consistently opposed cropping.

I was consequently delighted to be invited by the Game Department to watch their cropping team in action. Bob Langeveld is now in charge of field operations and is making a very efficient job of it.

Bob was trained as an analytical chemist-assayer in South Africa but the routine of a lab was not exciting enough for him, so he left a promising career to take up hunting. After cropping hippo and doing some free-lance hunting in Uganda Bob joined my safaris for a season, taking out wilderness trail clients and filling in as a white hunter. I therefore know him fairly well and had every confidence in his skill. He has his share of the essential qualities for such a dangerous job: a lot of guts and the ability to shoot straight and remain cool in a tight spot. Strangely enough his training as a chemist also comes into good use, for the darting and drugging of wild animals in Africa today has become a highly developed technique. In the case of elephant culling, where the purpose is to kill the animal outright, there is no great problem for a generous overdose of a drug like S.S.C. (succinyl choline chloride) would be lethal regardless of where the dart strikes. Whereas if you intend to immobilise elephants temporarily for the purpose of marking them, as Bob has to do from time to time, another drug would be used and a far more critical dosage needed. The margin of error is even narrower with antelopes. In this case a dose large enough to put them out is required but not enough to kill them. Once the animal has been immobilised it must be injected with a tranquilliser drug to counteract the shock, for some species are very susceptible to shock after rough handling and would otherwise die if such a sedative were not administered. Having suffered the indignities of being darted, tied up and tagged, the poor animal has to have yet another needle containing an antibiotic which prevents complications setting in and a final one containing the antidote which brings it round to normal. Worse than being a recruit in the Army!

Drugs vary considerably in their effect on different animals. What is effective for one species may have quite different results in the case of another. A lot, too, depends on the animal's body weight, which has to be assessed before the dart is fired. Any underestimate would result in the ratio of drug to body weight being disproportionate and could prove fatal. The effects also vary according to where the dart enters the body. Research and experiments are still being carried out in this field in several places in Africa and the whole technique is at the experimental stage. But that is a problem for the back-room boys; Bob's problem that particular day was to kill elephants with a drug which had been amply tested and proved effective during several years of use in the field.

I called on him early on the day of our outing and found him preparing syringes for the dart gun. Wearing rubber gloves he was measuring out precisely, on to a delicate balance scale, eight grammes of a white powder-like substance, which I learnt was succinyl choline chloride. Each measure was dissolved in 15 c.c. of distilled water and carefully poured into the front end of a fearsome looking syringe, the cylinder of which was about six inches long with a tough hypodermic needle about the same length. It is this syringe that is fired from the dart gun. The syringe has a diminutive cartridge inside which detonates on impact, forcing the plunger down and thus injecting the drug into the animal.

There was no need to read the printed warning on the canisters. I could see by the look of concentration on Bob's face and the meticulous way he was handling this substance that it was deadly poisonous. The slightest trace of the drug in a scratch or open wound would be instantly fatal. No antidote is known. It is not the sort of thing to leave lying around on Grandma's bedside table!

Bob's team that day consisted of himself, Rice, who is a first-class African hunter and a thoroughly reliable back-up gun, and M'tonga, an excellent tracker and bushman who was Bob's gun-bearer. I was there purely as an observer and carried no arms. The four of us piled into Bob's Land-Rover, which is specially modified for the work he is doing. The cab and windscreen had been stripped down and a fairly stout hand-rail had been built in the back on which was mounted a powerful searchlight. The rail allowed Bob's assistants to stand up and hold on whilst travelling over rough ground and the searchlight was for hunting at night. It has been found that the only satisfactory way to crop hippo is at night, when they come up on land to feed. During the day hippo are usually to be found in deep water and although it would not be impossible to shoot them in the pools the recovery of the carcasses would present quite a problem.

But our object today was elephant. We were travelling in the Game Reserve down the 05 towards the Luwi River. The 05 is a cropping road running more or less north and south – in fact on a compass bearing of 05 degrees, as the name suggests – which is used as a base-line for cropping operations in the reserve. By building its own road network away from the river the Game Department is able to crop without interfering with tourist game-viewing in the riverine area.

We had passed a lot of game on our way, including a party of half-a-dozen elephants before we reached the cropping area. Two miles before the Luwi we came across a small herd of cow elephants with calves of various sizes. This was a typical family group which had to be sacrificed in the cause of habitat protection. We stopped in the shade of a large cordyla tree and Bob switched on his transmitter set to contact Jack Botha, manager of the Cropping Unit, who controls the abattoir and cold-storage factory and was responsible for organising the recovery of the animals killed by Bob's team.

Bob was saying in his precise clipped South African accent: 'AZ four three to AZ four zero . . . AZ four three to AZ four zero . . . do you read me?'

After repeating this call sign half-a-dozen times AZ40 decided to come in: 'AZ four zero to AZ four three . . . am reading you loud and clear . . . pass your message.'

Bob's jargon became less mechanical when he felt he was talking to a person rather than the ether. 'Morning Jack, sorry to awaken you from your deep sleep but some of us have a job to do and as you're the boss I thought I'd keep in touch.'

Jack was used to Bob's ribbing but refused to let him get

away with it. 'Listen, Langeveld, don't talk to me about sleeping – I've been up since 5.30 trying to get that blasted generator working and I noticed you weren't up then. Anyway, pass your report.'

'O.K. I'm on the 05 two miles short of the Luwi. I'm going in after a bunch of cows and calves just east of this point. If I have no luck with this lot I will continue west up the Luwi. Will you instruct Recovery to proceed to the cross-roads at the 18-mile peg and wait my further instructions there?'

'Roger, I've got your message,' which Jack repeated meticulously. 'O.K., Bob. Report back to me when the first load is on its way and I'll get the factory labourers standing by. If that is all from you this is four zero signing off, over and out. Good luck!'

By this time the elephants had moved off out of sight but we had no difficulty picking up their tracks. M'tonga, as tracker, was in front, although the occasion did not call for much tracking skill, and he was followed by Bob and Rice. I was bringing up the rear and trying to be inconspicuous so as not to interfere with their freedom of manœuvre. We caught up with the herd in fairly open stunted woodland as they moved along browsing from tree to tree in a fairly compact group.

When we first sited the herd Bob handed over his double ·470 rifle to M'tonga and took over his dart gun. From the satchel he was carrying he took out one of the syringes he had so carefully prepared an hour or so previously and loaded it into his dart gun.

The wind was in our favour and Bob did not waste any time. He walked up to within about twenty yards of the leading cow and shot a dart into her flank. The slight explosion from the ·22 blank cartridge which propels the dart was hardly loud enough to disturb the herd but when Bob had first walked up

Bob Langeveld, a Government Cropping Ranger, is seen in action
with a dart gun. Below, one of the herd decided to retaliate and he had
to use an ordinary rifle to drop it at point blank range

Cropping team in action. Culling surplus elephant population is necessary to save the habitat and prevent the conditions seen in an earlier illustration

Towards dusk elephants leave the sanctuary of the reserve to go down to the Luangwa. After dark they feed in the thinly populated area on the other side, returning at dawn to the reserve. It will be interesting to see if cropping in the reserve changes this habit to them boldly in the open their first reaction appeared to be surprise and it took some time before they registered alarm and mustered into a defensive phalanx. By this time Bob had already placed his first dart and M'tonga had rushed up and handed over his rifle in exchange for the dart gun which had to be reloaded. All this activity right under their bellies now frightened the group, which stampeded off in panic, squealing and demonstrating as they went. The darted elephant, who was obviously the leader, ran off strongly with the others and they all regrouped and took up a defensive stand a couple of hundred yards away. They were performing in a most spectacular way – ears out, trunks up, and emitting that shrill ear-piercing scream of theirs. Every now and again one of the adult cows would make a mock charge for ten or a dozen yards but seemed to lack the courage to push it home. She would then retreat, taking the remainder of the herd with her, and make a stand farther on. Bob, armed with his reloaded dart gun and followed by his two assistants, was in hot pursuit and I saw another dart strike into the flank of the second cow. By this time, not much more than a couple of minutes from the first encounter, the lead cow which was first darted was lagging. Her hind legs collapsed and she fell to the ground. The rest of the herd gathered round and were reluctant to move on. During the time it took us to catch up again the second darted cow was down and the others were all bunched around her.

The normal procedure when an elephant is darted with this particular drug is to sever the jugular artery whilst the heart is still beating, in order to bleed the meat for marketing. After the drug has taken effect and paralysis sets in the heart will continue to beat for about six minutes and it is during this time, before the heart stops, that the pumping action evacuates most of the blood from the body. If this is not done the carcass is less likely to be passed by the meat inspector back at the abattoir, where rigid rules of inspection and hygiene are applied.

S.S.C. belongs to the decamethonium group of muscle relaxants and breaks down into harmless sugars which are absorbed into the muscle tissues. This drug (and its sister derivatives) has been in use in the medical profession for some time in surgery, where it is desirable to obtain complete muscle relaxation without many of the side-effects resulting from the use of more conventional anaesthetics. The effect of the drug in the massive overdose which Bob uses is to block off the nerve synapses causing a total muscular paralysis; the animal normally dies of suffocation due to collapse of the lungs.

Bob is not entirely satisfied that an elephant so anaesthetised still cannot feel pain when its throat is cut, so to make sure he finishes it off with a 9-mm. Parabellum automatic pistol, which he carries in a holster at his hip. The heart still beats on for a minute or two but the animal is instantly killed from a point-blank brain shot.

This is straightforward enough provided you can get to the drugged animal to give it the *coup de grâce*, but when the rest of the herd see their leaders lying down when they would normally be making the decisions they lose all sense of purpose and simply hang around waiting for someone to take the initiative. This makes for the kind of confused and panic-stricken situation which faced Bob at that moment. With his ·470 cradled in the crook of his arm he approached in the open to within about thirty yards and waved his arm and shouted at the elephants, hoping to drive them off so he could deal with the two on the ground. This was too much for one of the cows and she made a determined charge straight at Bob. There is no mistaking the real thing, and this was it. When an elephant is bluffing and makes a mock charge there is something phoney about it that is difficult to describe but becomes discernible with experience. On the other hand, when it really means business it cuts out all the preliminaries like demonstrating and trumpeting and just charges. It is a magnificent but frightening experience to have to face up to.

This was one of those charges. Bob waited for the elephant to get within a dozen yards, then put her down with a brain shot from his double ·470. The momentum of her movement carried her on a few more yards and she covered Bob in a shower of dust and flying grit as she fell.

We continued our operation until the sun was well overhead and by midday there were twenty-one elephant carcasses on low-loaders on their way to the abattoir. This represents a great loss of animal life, I admit, but if I have made my point and convinced the reader that cropping is necessary, then I am happy to know that at least this is being done efficiently and with as little suffering as possible.

EPILOGUE

21. A final reckoning

When I look back on a lifetime spent mostly in or on the fringes of wildlife sanctuaries in Africa, I feel I must try and draw up a mental balance sheet. In one column I must put the loss of human companionship and the sacrifices one has to make when one deliberately excludes oneself from the benefits of a gregarious society. Also on the debit side, my conscience reminds me to put those phases early in my career when hunting became an obsession and I killed more elephants and buffalo than was absolutely necessary. The animals had not yet become more important to me as species than as a medium for expressing my prowess.

On the other hand, I think I should give myself credit for my part in the formation of several sanctuaries in Northern Rhodesia (now Zambia) and my contribution towards many conservation projects; I have helped draft legislation and influence new policies; I have helped to establish one of Africa's largest national parks, and became the first Warden of it. I have worked to encourage interest in these reserves and to teach the emergent African people, upon whose shoulders the responsibility now lies, the value of their wildlife resources.

One does not do these things alone; one is part of a team of people imbued with the same desire to conserve the wonderful wildlife with which we have been so generously endowed. The results of these efforts are not always apparent, and the extent of one's contribution can only be assessed in the light of history. I hope that when the final reckoning is made the influence I have been able to assert will show a credit balance in my favour.

But apart from these mundane considerations there are other, more aesthetic, rewards to be gleaned from a lifetime spent in out-of-the-way places, and these will always remain with me.

I have sat in the shade of a magnificent evergreen trichelia on the banks of the Luangwa River and watched the impala come down to drink, materialising from the shadows one by one on the far bank as though by spontaneous creation; I have watched a skein of sacred ibis, in perfect arrow formation, flying down a river which the setting sun has turned to a shimmer of molten gold; I have seen a magnificent kudu bull on an anthill, silhouetted against the dawn sky; I have smelt the fragrant scent of the wild shrubs at sundown, when the world hesitates before handing over to the lords of darkness; I have lived with the night noises – the eerie plaintive call of the hyena, crying with the pathos of a lost soul in purgatory, and the music of the King of Beasts proclaiming his undisputed rule over his domain; I have seen a pure white impala.

All these and many other idyllic memories return to me and I cannot help but contrast them with the turmoil of Regent Street in the rush hour.

I know I have no regrets.